Dedicated to:

HETEROSEXUAL MEN EVERYWHERE
(The civilized type)
LONG MAY THEY MULTIPLY AND
BE AMONG US

Contents

Final Thoughts

First published in Great Britain by Bret Publications 1986
Reprinted 1993

Copyright © Bret Publications 1986

ISBN 0 9511442 0 0

Set in Linotron Palatino
Printed and Bound in Great Britain

How to Handle a Man

In English
[as she is spoken]

How to Handle Men!

The art of handling men is just that – an art – a technique that takes most of us females a lifetime of study and experience to acquire. By the time most of us have learnt a trick of two, we're ready to settle for a quiet life, with Shep the dog, as our companion, and only an occasional fling at Bingo for excitement.

In Japan, Geisha girls, I'm told go through a rigid training course to learn how to pamper and pander to the male ego; weary businessmen go to them to be flattered, to be relaxed, also entertained, when the troubles and cares of this world, prove too heavy for their frail systems. I know of no similar arrangement for females, but then its hardly surprising is it – it's a man's world.

Some girls are fortunate to be born with that instinctive knowledge, of how to cope with the male species: charm, personality, good looks, whatever it is, these fortunate girls have a flair for getting the best out of the male. For the rest of us, it's the 'hit 'n miss' trial and error method, finding out in the school of hard knocks.

This book is meant as a kind of guide-line for females of every age, in need of assistance, in this male dominated world, hopefully it will help you to handle your particular chauvinistic partner.

The very first thing to learn, to imprint upon your mind, is to write in large bold letters, on a fairly large piece of cardboard, then hang it or pin it up, in the kitchen, bathroom or bedroom, where you will see it several times a day.

MEN ARE MADE DIFFERENTLY FROM WOMEN!

Obvious? of course it is – but – how often do we actually remember the truth of those few words? They don't function like women. They don't think like women. It takes skill, it takes tact, it takes experience, it takes knowledge, it takes an awful lot of 'know now' to handle the male species, but there is one weapon that is quite indispensable, one you just cannot do without, it never fails, but must be used carefully, no skillfully, and that weapon is – flattery.

3

Here's an example, Henry Hodge lives at a seaside town. Has a thriving business, staff of twelve, he is the 'Boss'. Expects, wants, likes, plenty of attention. If its not forthcoming his moods become sulky, like a spoilt child.

Henry believes that colour with a capital 'C' is the answer to lots of life's little problems, and to prove his point, he turns up at his place of business, wearing a check jacket, maroon shirt, yellow tie, brown trousers, his favourite grey waistcoat, black shoes.

His Girl-Friday, knows the drill, its a well practised routine by now.

'Oh! Mr Hodge you've done it again, you look smashing, how do you do it?' That reaches Henry right in the gut; he smiles, pats his hair, smiles modestly, 'thank you, kind of you to say so – me dear, just a dash of colour here and there.'

'Well, you certainly brighten up a dull Monday morning Mr Hodge.' Just the right words, not too many, Pat knows how far to go, and now the Boss is in a good mood.

'Combining the right colours is an art Miss Merrick you either know how to, or you don't . . . take my wife now . . . we don't see eye to eye about colour, but then she's a bit of a square, you know traditional, conservative in taste . . . dull . . . that's what I call it.'

The day starts well, Henry feels good, next time Pat wants a day off, or extra shopping time, she gets it, Henry knows good secretaries are hard to come by.

So! everyone wins.

Henry Hodge goes home happy; his wife is glad to have her husband home, contented, so she's happy; Pat gets her perks; the staff can relax, so they're happy, everybody's happy – well nearly everyone.

The optician who plays golf with Henry hasn't the courage to tell him he's colour blind.

✱ ✱ ✱ ✱ ✱ ✱ ✱ ✱ ✱ ✱

Its a male disease this ego thing, found in males, in every strata of society.

Take Chris Murphy, he's the foreman at the factory where they make ladies underwear. Chris is good at his job, but he's thick as a plank. The factory girls shovel on the flattery, but he never twigs; Chris thinks he's the boy who puts joy into every heart, when he walks through the factory gates every morning.

He's a trendy fellow, our Chris, believes in keeping smack

up to date with fashion. His wife can wear last years' coat, but he has a duty to keep right in with the latest image; after all he has his appearance to think of, what would his girls at the factory think, if he didn't.

One Friday morning he turned up for work, all prepared for the big darts match that night – Chris was an important member of the team; he had a hair-do, that no self respecting gorilla, lying in a taxidermist, waiting to be stuffed – would be caught dead in.

Chris is a bit on the short side, and his hairdresser had gone overboard; well, either that, or he held a grudge against Chris. He had a bouffant style, which had been teased, back-combed, lacquered into a high dome effect, and although wearing raised heels, Chris had to duck in the fairly high doorway, to get into the showroom.

'Chris' shrieked Gladys, the dragon in charge . . . 'you've been to Vidal Sassoon, wow! aren't you the trendiest trick in the town . . . get a whiff of that perfume . . . no . . . no . . . let me guess . . . its Soir de Paris? no . . . its . . . its Brute . . . oh Chris you are a knockout . . .'

She does a dance around him, admiring his 'threads', his sideburns, she's no fool our Gladys. 'Hey girls' . . . goes to the workroom door . . . 'come and get a load of our Chris, oh you'll knock 'em dead at the match tonight, shouldn't be surprised to see you on the telly . . . right girls . . .'

They get the nod from Glad, and troop in showering praises on Chris, sniffing his after-shave and he's happy, happy, basking in this chorus of female approval.

The fact that he looks like a reject from Star Wars, and stinks like a liberated faggot, doesn't enter his thick skull; he knows his girls are true-blue, and always fair in their judgement.

Chris is a 24 carat chauvinistic pig. Nothing can dent his ego, his wife's criticisms float right off him, he puts it down to jealousy, his girls know best, a good lot they are too, on the whole.

Mind you they do take advantage of his good nature, sometimes they go a bit too far over tea-breaks, leaving early, he will have to talk to them severely about that, but that is tomorrow's problem, and it can wait.

Today he must make sure he doesn't get his hair messed up, I mean, he just could be on the telly . . . yeah . . . better buy a fine hair-net, just in case.

Life's full of little problems............!!!

◉ ◉ ◉ ◉ ◉ ◉ ◉ ◉ ◉ ◉

How to Remain a Virgin!

Virgins have always been special. Set apart from the rest of us mortals, they have a unique place in history, since way, way back.

The most famous of all was The Virgin Mary. Then, there were the 'Vestal Virgins' who lived in a Greek temple. They were especially hand-picked, pretty, pure, untouched. They spent their entire lives in seclusion, dancing, frolicking, playing music, protected and guarded by huge eunuchs.

No man was allowed near them, the Head Priest saw to that. No sneaking off at night, for a quick pasta, a glass of oozoo, with Nick the Greek, over a candle-lit dinner. No sir! They were Vestal Virgins, all of them prized possessions, their lives dedicated to serving the Gods, and no one else.

I personally don't think that is the ideal way for a pretty young maiden to finish up her days, closeted with a bunch of other females, but, there are worse ways to go.

For example, even today a virgin is very much sought after in Middle East countries. They advertise discreetly, but you would have to be knowledgeable to understand the cryptic messages put in the paper, or you would miss the meaning entirely.

In the 'Saudi Sentinel' you'd read something like this:

'Fresh, new parthenogenetic model wanted, vintage, around 16. Will negotiate price'.

Translation:

Young virgin, sixteen years old, will pay up to 100 barrels of oil, one 1986 Mercedes, 50 head of cattle, Flat on Costa-del-Sol.

So you see its very important to guard your gift, to value yourself. Put yourself on a pedestal, you'll be appreciated and offers will come your way.

The biggest problem in this day and age of permissiveness for many young girls, is how to hang on to that special gift, you are supposed, by tradition, to hand over to your lawfully

7

wedded husband, on the bridal night, it takes a very clever maiden to reach the altar these days, with undamaged goods, so to speak.

In Spain or South America, they still have duennas', but here there is no such thing, chances are if you have a chaperon in Britain, the old girl is so lively, more than ready to enjoy a fling herself, that a young virgin ends up chaperoning the chaperon. So the big question remains, what can a nice young girl do in an awkward situation to protect herself?

First, engrave upon your mind, one fact.

NO MAN CAN BE TRUSTED not a one, as long as you remember this and repeat it daily, you will have some measure of protection.

Men will trick you, they will deceive you, charm you, and entice you, there is nothing they won't stoop to do to get their own way. They'll make any promise. A trip in one of Freddie Laker's old planes, help with your weekend chores, one fellow went as far as buying his date's mother a gin 'n tonic, they will lie, do anything to deflower you, so, what CAN a young girl in love do to remain pure, who does not want to go in for a heavy petting session?

There is a way to protect yourself. Just follow instructions. Take an ordinary scene, in any town, of two young people in love. It's early summer and the night is made for lovers, you sit together on a river-bank, or in a car high above the town in Lover's Lane.

The countryside is bathed in silvery moonlight, its fairy-like, almost unreal, the night filled with sweet, throbbing romance and your lover filled with throbbing ideas. The stars twinkle above, his kisses make you weak, your knees turn to jelly at his slightest touch, you are at your most vulnerable, his dark eyes smoulder with passion, his lips tender and loving, he whispers sweet words into your ears. How can a mere girl, inexperienced resist this, oh, so experienced seducer?

Most of us virgins have found ourselves in this sort of situation some time or another, when the senses are reeling, when speech is obsolete and he is using braille for communication. What to do? How to control this seductive invasion upon your senses, your body?

The answer is relatively simple.

Just when you are going, going, gasping for air, almost into his evil clutches, when you know passion will take over, take a deep breath, push him away from you, sit upright, say lightly

8

almost casually, 'Georgie, do you think there's any chance of Tony Benn ever becoming Prime Minister?'

The effect of this remark, when passion is at its peak, could put him in a state of total shock, he'll sober up instantaneously. No one could possibly think of Tony Benn and remain passionate. He's much like Granny's long drawers, both guaranteed to kill all thoughts of hot-blooded desire. While he is trying to recover from this cold – matter-of-fact statement, you'll be in charge once again, and on your way home, still pure and unsullied.

Men never change, just keep on reminding yourself. They are not, I repeat, not, to be trusted. Selfish and devious, they are the old chauvinistic enemy, no matter how much they charm, or flatter, or tempt or coax.

Take the case of Lily Finch, married, settled so she thought into a routine, but when Eddie, her old man used to say, 'Now come on Lil, settle down, time for Coronation St'. What the old buzzard meant was, Elsie Tanner turned him on, and later that night, it would be passion night in Paddington, so Lily got smart.

Eddie's big hobby was greyhounds. She had a bit of money saved up, and after shopping around bought him a greyhound. Nothing pedigree mind you, just a run of-the-mill old dog. Well, Eddie was tickled pink. He exercised the dog, he started to attend meetings, he was out almost every night, and so busy with his new hobby, he never bothered with 'Coronation St' again, well, not seriously, he didn't even notice when Elsie Tanner left.

Lil now sees her favourite programmes in peace, as she said, 'You've got to think ahead, be one step in front when you live with your man . . . otherwise they'll step all over you.'

So, hang on to your virtue. Take a good hard look at the chap you're dating, don't be tempted or bribed, by an offer of a year's supply of diet Pepsi or Coca-Cola, or he might say he can get you dog biscuits at discount prices. That's an old trick, trying to get to you through your pet.

Be firm, stay pure, a long engagement never hurt anyone. Go to the altar dressed in white, a vision of loveliness, and, a virgin. But, I do suggest you read up about the 'birds 'n the bees', before your wedding night, unlike the innocent, young bride, who visited a large city hotel for the first time on her wedding night.

'We are newly-weds, and we would like a suite', said the groom to the hotel clerk.

'Bridal?' enquired the hotel clerk.

'Oh no'! blurted out the bride, 'I'll just hang on to his ears, until I get used to it'.

⊙ ⊙ ⊙ ⊙ ⊙ ⊙ ⊙ ⊙ ⊙ ⊙ ⊙

Grandmother –
Doing it Her Way

If I could have a special wish granted, I'd want to float back in time and talk with some of the outstanding women who gave so much colour to the past.

I'd start with Cleopatra and work my way through history calling upon Elizabeth I, then Nel Gwynne, Madame du Pompadour, visiting with a few other great ladies of France; then over to Russia and chat with the Great Dame, Catherine the Great, what a earful I'd get about men from her, but one female not recorded in history would be a lady I just barely remember, my mother's mother, Magdalene, now there was a dame if ever there was one!

Magdalene lived long before any modern contraption like the telephone or radio, TV and the like, polluted the joy of every-day living, she had four husbands, was planning yet another trip to the alter, when God in his infinite wisdom looked down and called a halt, and Magdalene went home, enjoying no doubt the company of a few male angels, for wherever she is, there are sure to be admirers.

Grandmother was born and lived her entire life in a small rural Welsh village. Horses were the main form of transport: Church and chapel was the heart, the very centre of village life and activity. Women wore long skirts reaching down to the ankle, and a trip to the seaside, just twenty miles away was an annual event, eagerly discussed and looked forward to, months before this joyous occasion happened, the anticipation apparently was quite incredible, enough food and drink was prepared and packed to accommodate a full battalion of soldiers, but life was simple and pleasures homemade.

Farming was what occupied and provided for most families, everyone helped his neighbour to cut the hay, store it, everyone grew vegetables and fruit, competitions for the biggest marrow or the best apples, or whatever, was an enjoyable occasion, with singing and feasting on home-made grub, washed down by home-made wines. Life was hard, simple,

11

but very rich and rewarding too in human relationships; everyone knew everyone, loneliness was quite unheard of, walking was a necessity, chapels were full every Sunday, giving everyone a chance to indulge in the two favourite forms of entertainment, a good gossip and the opportunity to sing.

Magdalene was petite of form, attractive rather than pretty, her best feature was her beautiful eyes – she had a lively personality, quick wit and she made no bones of the fact that she preferred the company of men to women, a compliment that was returned in full measure by the men, much to the chagrin and envy of the other village girls.

Careful of her figure – Magdalene's waist measurement was 22" all her life, she was a born coquette; she had, I'm told, a favourite little trick, when talking with a man, she would look down at her shoes or study her hands, then without warning abruptly look up giving her admirer the full blast of her green slanted eyes which apparently set a man's heart thumping in exquisite agony, a practised piece of feminine coquetry she thoroughly enjoyed.

Grandmother's first husband was a Morgan: the second a Griffiths: the third an Edwards: and the fourth was another Morgan. She wed her first when she was but a girl, enjoyed wedded bliss until a tragic accident ended this idyllic union, she was a widow, shortly before her nineteenth birthday.

No sooner had relatives and friends left, and the remains of the huge feast cleared away, it was the custom of the day to offer a sumptuous meal after the funeral, and sixty was a normal crowd, people walking great distances to pay their last respects – well no sooner had Magdalene washed the dishes, returned those that had been borrowed from family to accommodate so many hungry mouths, than, a village man would come knocking on her door, usually the back door, away from prying eyes, offering to chop wood, fetch in the coal, or wanting to mend the garden fence, thus enraging and infuriating the spinsters of the village, who saw in Magdalene a threat to their own chances of being 'taken off the shelf' – a stigma worse than a dose of clap.

But Magdalene went her merry way and before the year was out, she was once again married and warm in her matrimonial bed.

Through no fault of my grandmother's after a happy six years of wedded bliss Griffiths a strong healthy man, was struck by lightning and once again dressed in black, which

13

was most becoming to her Magdalene cried and then once again turned to the business of living.

Her next husband lasted out for twenty years, whatever her secret regarding men, every husband had that look of bliss on his face, they all apparently adored Magdalene, waited upon her hand and foot, would be seen doing 'unmanly' things like carrying big parcels or helping her down from a high step of the horse 'n trap – Magdalene firmly believed that life without a male to sweeten the days and nights, was a total waste of being a woman, and she for one didn't intend to be without this small comfort.

When Edwards died of a heart attack, the spiteful spinsters said it was because she wore 'em out in bed, but she wed Josh Morgan before the year was out and settled, naturally easily into 'the old routine'.

Grandmother Morgan had very definite ideas about the man and woman relationship, here are a few of her comments.

'Men are by nature peacocks, they like to strut, preen themselves, some are pompous, others arrogant, some down right impossible – but – they ARE the boss, you will not change that, so what you can't change, you come to terms with.'

'Sit down and listen to your man. Give him a hot meal when he comes home tired. Don't load him down with complaints and troubles when he walks in through the door. He's come home to shut out the world, make it a haven, let him think he is the wisest man in the world, no matter how big a fool he is, he's *your* man, bring out the best in him, and he'll be your slave for life.'

'Take time every day to make him feel important, make him feel good. Make him king on his own hearth, if he's had a rough time outside, let him know at home he's No. 1 it's his castle. Soothe him, stroke him, pet him, spoil him, let him know you admire him, he'll appreciate you more than gold, and forever put you first in his life.'

Just a few little things that Magdalene Morgan – Griffiths – Edwards – Morgan felt were important in handling men, it worked with four husbands and would have probably worked with another four, we'll never know, I suppose there's a message somewhere . . .

⊙ ⊙ ⊙ ⊙ ⊙ ⊙ ⊙ ⊙ ⊙ ⊙ ⊙

Pests

The male pest inhabits every strata of society. He's found in pubs, clubs, in quiet neighbourhoods, offices, hospitals, everywhere where men and women work or gather to socialize, you'll find the male pest at work. He's been likened to the garden slug, not without reason. He creeps silently, crawls without a sound and always when he thinks there's no chance of being discovered.

An acquaintance of mine, Angela and her husband used to frequent a country Inn on weekends. One of their 'crowd', we'll call him Mark, was part of their group. He and his wife Cynthia, were always there Friday evening, Saturday evening and Sunday noon.

Mark, a nattily dressed lecher, made it plain to Angela he fancied her and joked about it to Tim her husband. At the bar he'd manage to sit next to her, he'd put his hand on her thigh, reach across in a way that made contact with her breasts and in a dozen ways pestered her. When she told Tim he simply laughed, saying old Mark fancied every pretty bird.

Occasionally she was forced to dance with him as part of the group, she couldn't without making a scene, avoid doing so. The weekends became a nightmare. Nothing she could say stopped him. She would sit as far away as possible, but he'd smile a hail-fellow-well-met greeting, then move near when the appropriate moment presented itself. There was no way she could avoid him, he worked quietly, smiling, always when the others were chatting or busy.

Cynthia his wife loved male company, she flirted with the others, drank, and appeared not to notice what her husband was up to.

One Saturday night it was the annual golf dinner. A 4-star affair with dancing, a floor show, all the crowd looked forward to it. The girls in their glamour outfits, the fellows in tuxedo. Angela dreaded the hours ahead, her husband Tim refused to listen to her complaints. Tim thought the best about everyone and felt she was exaggerating the whole thing.

Everyone sat together as usual at one table, old friends sharing memories, conversing with the comfortable ease of

people with shared confidences, who have entertained each other in their homes. The good food, the wine, the music, atmosphere relaxed everyone. Mark asked Angela for a dance, she refused making some excuse. Biding his time Mark waited, then later with a big smile asked her again. this time Tim made her go, 'Go on Angie, give Romeo his dance, he won't leave your alone until he gets one.'

Reluctantly she stepped on the floor, the multi-coloured lights from a thousand pieces of mirror, darkened the floor and Mark took advantage. He held her tight, practically chewed her ear, suggested a motel, his hands busy, it was the same dialogue as before, she ignored him, and eventually the dance ended.

Around midnight the party now in full swing, Tim was at the bar talking golf, the others dancing or telling jokes, Angela made her way to the 'Ladies'. Through the hall, along a short corridor, past the small lounge. On her way back he was waiting. Mark grabbed her by the elbow, pushed her onto a settee in the lounge, his hands moving faster than a bookie at the races. She pushed him away, tried to, but was no match for this six-foot athlete. He held her down, tearing at the top of her dress, she struggled, bit his lip, it must have hurt but he wouldn't let her go, he was like someone gone beserk.

Then with super-human effort she wrenched herself away, got up but not quick enough he grabbed her again, but by now all the past slimy actions of this creep seemed to flash before her eyes. Without hesitation, she lifted her right knee and with strength she didn't know she had, gave him such a punch between his legs, he fell back yelling in agony. Angela walked away, straightening her hair, adjusting her dress.

The outcome was predictable. Mark, unable to face anyone called a cab and went home. Later he and his wife moved away from the district, they never spoke to Angela or Tim again, and one pest was removed from one club, because one wife had taken all she could.

Unfortunately this breed of pest is not exclusive to Britain.

I spent some time in Arkansas not too long ago. It's one of the prettiest, yet least known parts of the United States and gets very hot in summer.

My friends had a domestic help, only they aren't called that in Little Rock, 'domestic mechanics', very grand but doing the same work as a charlady. This one was called Belle, a stout, tough aggressive black woman, who had no qualms about

17

interrupting a conversation, or joining in if she felt like it without invitation.

One morning my hostess had a few friends over for lunch, an early brunch affair. We were discussing men, one in particular who was a problem, a pest and how to get rid of him, when the 'domestic mechanic' Belle, sat herself down and said, 'Now they ain't no real problem them pests, they is only trash an' trash you has to get rid of fast. Like ma daughter Marie, she had a problem with trash, but she got rid of it.'

We urged her to tell us, not that she needed any urging.

Her daughter Marie lived in the best part of the black residential area, recently married, her husband was on the road a great deal, but her neighbours were friendly and helpful, one husband much too friendly.

Vernon Blott was a contractor, ran his own business, his wife worked in a real estate office and was out all day. They had no children, been married for ten years and Marie found Vernon dropping in casually to see if she needed anything, was 'alright' just considerate because her husband was out of town.

At first she offered him coffee, but when she became aware that his attention was mostly on her trim body, she realized his intentions and quickly tried to curtail any further visits, she locked the kitchen door, but the summer heat made the house so hot she was forced to open it again? Vernon wasn't easily put off, he'd knock with ice-cream, a basket of strawberries, making it impossible to be rude, and naturally she would have to invite him to share the fruit and ice-cream. He'd be fast on his feet to help her get the dishes out, brushing close to her, any excuse to put their bodies close together. Marie felt dreadful but helpless, he wasn't doing anything, yet she knew what he was after, the naked admiration in his eyes told it all.

One day visiting her mother Belle asked why she looked so 'pe-ak-d' 'Ain't you eatin' proper chile?' she asked. Marie said she was fine, but eventually Belle got the whole story from her. The old battle-axe was all for going back with her daughter and flattening Vernon with her fists, she had the equipment to do it too, but Marie told her 'No,' she wanted no trouble, she had to live with her neighbours and in peace, she'd find a way.

Belle brooded on this problem, then she hit on an idea.

Next day, Belle turned up at Marie's home with a cake box in her hands and who should knock on the door mid-morning, but Vernon.

Marie introduced him and Belle was all sweetness itself, she produced the coffee cake freshly baked, 'Why that's ma favourite kinda cake,' said Vernon, 'ah can never git enough.'

Belle smiled at him, 'Today you kin eat all your little heart fancies . . . now Marie here, she don't care for nothing sweet, a salad girl, that's my Marie.'

They chatted amicably with Vernon drinking three cups of coffee and four big slices of coffee cake, had he taken time to notice he would have observed Belle didn't eat any of it.

Then abruptly Vernon, clutching his stomach, got up, 'Excuse me,' and he rushed out of the house. Marie looked puzzled, but Belle picked up the rest of the cake and threw it in the dustbin. Marie asked her why he did that, but Belle shrugged her shoulders and shortly left.

Marie didn't see or hear from Vernon for two weeks, indeed it was almost three when she did see him and he just casually nodded at her and walked away, she wasn't bothered again.

Belle chuckling and looking pleased told us, 'We did hear latah that his doctah did say, it was one of de worse cases of diarrhoea he did evah come across!'

⊙ ⊙ ⊙ ⊙ ⊙ ⊙ ⊙ ⊙ ⊙ ⊙

Bald Men and Wigs

Its always a bit of a tragedy, when a man, especially a young man, starts to lose his hair; but, when the chips are down, it's the character, the personality of the man himself that counts, not the amount of fuzz on top of his head.

In some cases a wig does improve the appearance. Movie buffs, can spot the difference in many film heroes, who a couple of decades ago, showed signs of a thinning top and today sport a well groomed thatch, thanks to skilful art work. However, if a man won't spend real money on a good wig, he is apt to draw a lot of attention to himself, and not always, complimentary.

There is also, the myth, or the legend, take your choice, that men with bald heads are more virile, passionate than their hirsute brothers, I wouldn't know about that.

My first contact with an artificial top happened many years ago, when I was a child. Brought up in a small country village, our tastes and pleasures were simple indeed. Mothers, Aunties, Grandmothers baked and sewed most of our necessities, home-made jams, cakes, bread, indeed very little was 'shop-bought'.

One of my Aunts, fearful of having that most dreaded of all stigma attached to her, 'left on the shelf', went about trapping, enticing, and indeed capturing the only bachelor for miles around.

One could hardly call, Dai Evans eligible, and by no stretch of the imagination, good-looking. Dai was short, at least a head shorter, than my Auntie Flo, he was very, very, bow-legged, and a good sport. When he came a-courting Auntie, and she would be in the parlour putting lavender water on her hankie, we kids, would get Spot the dog to jump through his legs, in 'n out, he didn't mind, provided he had a glass of rhubarb wine, very partial was Dai to a drop of home-made wine.

As long as I can remember Dai wore a wig. Apparently he started to lose his hair, early in life, by the time he was thirty, most of it was around his ears, or, as old Dan the barber, a

21

kindly old soul would say, 'Yewer not losing yewer hair Dai bach, just gaining more face.'

Early one summer's day, Dai and a crowd of the local lads, caught the milk-train, and off they went to London, to watch their team play the English at football. A tremendously important event then, when television hadn't even been thought of, and only the doctor had a telephone.

As is traditional with the football crowd, they drank their way steadily, from pub to pub, until they reached Paddington. Finding an extra half hour on their hands, they went into a second-hand shop, and browsed around, and there, propped up on a dusty top shelf was a wig, a shiny, curly, black wig.

'Hey . . . Dai . . .'ere a minute,' the chaps crowded around Iueun, as he put the wig upon Dai's shining pate. 'Dew mawr, look boys, what do you think of our Dai now?' Iueun, none too steady, was winking, making faces at the others. 'Smashing . . . hey . . . the girls won't leave you alone now Dai' much jollity, and the upshot was, that Dai parted with 15 shillings, borrowing 2/- and put it on.

From that day, Dai never took his wig off, except to sleep. First of all, fifteen bob, was a great deal of money, and he wasn't going to see it wasted, secondly it did keep his head warm, thirdly people were paying more attention to him.

True, Dai and his wig was the topic of conversation for weeks and weeks, partly because it was the wrong colour. Dai's natural colour hair was gingerish, he had light blue eyes, fair skin and the sight of the black, curly wig, shining, like a blackbird's wing, in contrast to his fair complexion came as a shock to those who knew him, it took time for the villagers to become accustomed to his odd appearance; but, familiarity soon makes the unusual common-place, and 'Dai the Wig' became a regular part of village life.

When the weather was really hot, his wig would shift around, either that or his head was shrinking. We kids referred to Dai, as the 'man whose hair moved'.

Mothers in the village, were not above making full use of Dai's topnotch, and to turn it to their advantage. Keeping the children quiet in chapel was an age old problem. Dai was a regular chapel goer. Mothers would get to chapel, extra early, sit in the pew behind Dai, and tell the children, that if they watched, very carefully, his hair would move. Stuffed with gob-stoppers, mintoes, chewy toffee, we kids would sit quietly eyes glued to the back of his head watching, not daring to speak, waiting to see if the black shining wig would move. It never did, not in our chapel anyway.

If your current escort is thinning on top, its well to be on guard against sudden outbursts, or a swift change of moods. Passion is very near the surface with this type of man, a sexy female can throw this chap completely off balance, and arouse fierce longings, buried deep down.

They have inexplicable, ungovernable moods. A small thing from a lovely lady can swiftly change a quiet man into what can only be compared to a demented bull moose, chasing his mate and I tell you truthfully, there is no more terrifying sight upon this earth, than a lustful bull moose in full pursuit of his mate.

Years ago, a friend of mine was dining with her current boy-friend in a New York restaurant. They ordered the speciality of the house – Spaghetti bolognaise, and a bottle of chianti, Peg and Hymie settled in for a happy evening. Peg was just putting a forkful of spaghetti to her mouth, when Hymie who had been watching her, as if mesmerized, jumped up, spilling sauce, meat-balls, wine and spaghetti all over the place said, 'Come on, we're going.' He grabbed her hand and with the other, put some dollar bills on the table. 'I'm mad about you let's go. . .'

She recognized the look of the wolf and said, 'OK . . . OK . . . but I must go to the little girls place first.' She managed to crawl out of a small window in the lavatory, scraped her legs, when falling several feet, grabbed a cab, got home, locked the door and took the phone off the hook. A narrow escape.

It's wise, when dining out with your topless gentleman friend, to try and be seated centre of the restaurant, where there are people all around you. Same thing in a theatre, cinema, you never know when the urge will hit this fellow.

Most of them are sensible, well behaved, but be warned, they don't have that tag, 'more virile than the rest' – for nothing.

My Aunt was a kind normal lady, yet Dai sired ten children. OK, there wasn't any television, but he was an active sports-man, enjoyed all kinds of activities; here are a few suggestions to help you when dating your fellow.

Wear dresses with high necklines. Lay off the perfume, with this highly sexed group, you must avoid stoking up the fires, perfume does just that. Wear ankle length skirts, they're back

23

in fashion again or trousers. NEVER wear anything with a zip, replace a zip with buttons.

If possible take a chaperon around with you, failing that do as Scotland Yard advises regarding burglars – same thing: 'Make it impossible for the thief to get your valuables.'

Bald headed men often make very good salesmen, quick witted and persuasive like this man.

The bald-headed barber was trying to sell his customer a bottle of hair tonic.

'How can you try and sell me a bottle when you have no hair yourself?' he was challenged.

'Nothing wrong with that,' was the answer.

'I know a guy who sells brassieres.'

◉ ◉ ◉ ◉ ◉ ◉ ◉ ◉ ◉ ◉ ◉

Tribal Types

The Welsh-man

The Celts are divided into two very different sectors, the 'Ancient Britons' the Welsh Celt, then you have the Irish Celt, but first let's talk about the 'Ancient Brit'.

* * * * * * * * * *

The voice of the Welshman is known throughout the world. Who hasn't heard of the most famous Welshman of the past decades, Richard Burton? The tributes paid to this man's speaking voice are legion. One Canadian paper wrote, 'Nowhere in the English speaking world has any man, Actor – Orator, Statesman, no-one can match the peerless beauty of his magical voice, every syllable a pearl of beauty . . .'

BOSTON, USA: 'He enchants, he enslaves, he charms, when he speaks he casts a spell upon man, woman, children . . .' and so many, many more tributes.

Two equally well-known, world reknown Welshman have done the same, but with their singing voices. Sir Geraint Èvans, has enchanted scores of millions with his voice and his charm. And of a younger vintage, but just as potent, just as lethal when it comes to wooing the females, we have Mr Tom Jones, these are but three, a sample of the Welsh male in action.

He's a spellbinder when he puts his mind to it he'll sing his maiden into submission if all else fails and if he can't sing he's in real trouble.

There is a movement afoot in Wales, to tax heavily the men who can't sing, failing that to deport them to England.

Discounting the uncouth, the slob, a minority fortunately in every race, when a Celt woos his maiden he gives his all – nothing! is held back. He courts his love in a fashion alien to the Scot, the Englishman. He gives his heart, his love, his body, if she'll take it and if that isn't enough, abandon drinking (for a very short season).

He will call upon his ancient forebears to pour their magic upon him. He'll burst into song, he'll run up mountains shouting to startled goats or sheep, that this love is bigger than

27

himself, a wondrous force filling his life with meaning and burning his insides, right clean down to his toes.

Morgan Jenkin, was so swept away on the tide of passion, that although known to be a very cautious man with a penny he went to Tillings the butcher and bought a tray on his succulent faggots (meat pies) had them gift-wrapped, rode his bike clean across into the next valley and delivered them to his heart's desire only to be told she was newly converted to becoming a vegetarian.

Quite undaunted Morgan Jenkin, rode off to the nearest haystack, scoffed the lot and had difficulty pushing his bike on the return journey home.

Drama of course, is part of the Celtic make-up. Flamboyant, reckless, moody, you never know where you are with your Celtic suitor, so its best to read up all you can about them, that is if you are new to the territory.

Especially if you are from Poland or Charlotte, North Carolina.

You can always expect the unexpected from Dai. He'll do things like ringing up at 2 a.m. You'll stumble out of bed, groping for the light, your mind full of thoughts about accidents or worse, only to find its him himself on the phone, 'It's me my lovely one, I couldn't sleep thinking about you. I've been to the bathroom three times already, my bowels are playing hell with me, my insides churning, burning . . . oh! if you were only here at my side my lovely one, I wouldn't need to go to the toilet every five minutes.'

Not exactly Shelley or Byron, but it does have a kind of primitive appeal. He'll write little rhymes (hardly Dylan Thomas vintage) and usually on the back of a betting slip, but it's from the heart.

The Welsh Celt is a chauvinistic creature with the odd exception. His attitude towards the female, is much like that of the Scot and the North Englishman. They are all chauvinistic pigs and consider women to be second class in brains, in equality, when familiarity takes over, the hunted captured and tamed this is revealed, but whilst the chase is on, charm, song, poetry, conceal the real nature of the man underneath.

He's cunning and wily, the Celt in pursuit, so be on your guard. My grandmother, who knew a thing or two about men used to pay a visit to the local herbalist, a euphemism for 'witch doctor'.

Down a leafy lane, right by the pigsty, until you reach a tiny cottage with dogs barking and daisies growing wild. She would cross the old crone's palm with gold – (silver went out with Henry VIII) and while you were waiting for the potion to be made up, drank a glass of Leek wine, after one glass of her wine you didn't care what happened.

Grandmother said, when her passionate suitor came a-calling, she'd sneak a tiny bit of the potion, rub it on the back of her neck, she said the combination of 'Soir de paris' [She used it by the pint] and the nectar worked like a dream. He became putty in her hands and that is where we females want them.

Nothing changes in human nature, it's all been done before. The same old tactics are tried, generation after generation, so do what girls have always done, turn the tables on the predator.

For example Dai, will pick you up in his car, for a romantic evening in a country Inn. Wales is full of small little Inns, updated with candle-light, music, soft carpets and very good food.

Chances are it's an Inn our Dai has used before, but you have come prepared too! Dressed in your prettiest blue cocktail outfit, earrings sparkling, you look perfect for that big night. But, you carry with you a large tin can, it looks very similar to a petrol can.

Dai will look very surprised to see a dainty little thing like you, all dolled up, with a tin can attached to your evening bag. 'What's this then,' a reasonable question. 'I'm prone to fainting fits, my doctor has given me oxygen, just in case.' 'I didn't know you fainted, you never told me.' Smile, a big smile. 'I didn't want to bother you with my problems.'

First hurdle over. After a perfect dinner in romantic surroundings, the next step is the usual, the car has run out of petrol, naturally, miles and miles from the nearest station.

Let him go through the routine, it's best not to accuse him outright. 'Would you credit it, I filled up the tank before we set out . . . there must be a leak, I shall have to take it to the garage tomorrow . . . meantime let's you and I get to know each other, my lovely . . .'

Produce your tin can, smile and give it to him, 'There you are, petrol, I had a feeling this just might happen, I only pretended about the oxygen.'

He might strangle you on the spot, an angry Celt is not a pretty sight, he just might make you walk home, or he might turn rough, in which case, get out that long hatpin and use it. If he laughs it off, you've found a chap who just could be worth cultivating.

29

Many a woman has married a Welsh Celt, and held her own.

Gwilym and Nesta had been married for a long, long time, they now were in the twilight years of their life. 89 and 84. One evening on a cold winter's night, seated at a roaring fire, they sipped their mugs of cocoa, reminiscing:

G: 'It's been a good, long life together, Nesta fach . . .'
N: 'Aye . . . we've had a good innings . . .'
G: 'Nesta there's something that's been pressing on my heart and any time now the Grim Reaper will call . . . I must get something off my chest . . .'
N: 'Yes . . . bach . . .'
G: 'Remember, the 1st World War, Nesta? . . .'
N: 'Yes Gwilym . . .'
G: I was unfaithful to you twice Nesta fach, once with Maggie Owen, and once with Beth Morgan, cashier at the Co-op . . . oh say you will forgive me cariad . . . please forgive me . . .' Looks pleadingly at wife.
LONG PAUSE.
N: 'I forgive you Gwilym . . .'
G: **EYES MISTY WITH GRATITUDE:** 'Thank you, thank you my girl . . . how is your cocoa . . . OK . . .'
N: 'It's fine . . . thank you Gwilym . . . **LONG PAUSE.** 'Talking about the war, World War 1 . . . Gwilym . . .'
G: 'Yes my girl . . .'
N: 'There's something I should tell you too . . .'
G: 'Whatever it is . . . you say it my lovely . . .'
N: 'I too was unfaithful to you Gwilym . . .
G: **ASTOUNDED:** 'Never! no . . .'
N: 'Twice Gwilym. Once with Bob Melish, and the other time with the Carmarthen Cavalry.'

Like all men with ego's, haven't they all, play up to your Celt. The one thing, they can't see clearly is flattery. The bigger the ego, the more you pour on the old soft soap.

Find his weakness. Soccer? His hair, appearance? His skill at gardening? Ask him questions compliment him, praise him, he'll soak it up, it's the only way, and it's a wonderful weapon, that we females have to counter attack with.

An old tried, tested, sure winner, is to get him to talk about himself. Get tanked up first and let him ramble on . . . it's good for a couple of hours at least.

The Welsh Celt is suspicious by nature. Especially of anything imported, like a girl from England, or overseas. He must be the 'boss', he's a male isn't he? That makes him automatically head of the house, decision maker, Top Dog. You'll find this attitude repeated in business, in social gatherings, at committee meetings, whenever the male and female come together, he, man, must be in charge.

Don't fight it, at least not with his weapons, use those you've been endowed with, they can be just as lethal and enormously effective.

Women are gaining ground, but slowly, it's an uphill battle getting fair play from a chauvinistic male world. However, help sometimes comes from an unexpected quarter.

The man had been brought to court for beating up his wife. On hearing the evidence the judge had pronounced him guilty.

'And,' added the judge, 'I fine you one hundred and ten pounds. The next time you think of beating your wife, you'll remember that it may be expensive.'

'I can understand the hundred pounds,' the man protested, 'but what's the ten pounds for?' 'That,' said the judge solemnly, 'is the entertainment tax.'

⊙ ⊙ ⊙ ⊙ ⊙ ⊙ ⊙ ⊙ ⊙ ⊙

The Irishman

The Irish Celt has many qualities similar to his Welsh counter-part. In temperament, his moods, love of drama, they are bro-thers under the skin, but Paddy is probably a shade more impetuous.

Paddy is the sort of man, when enveloped by the burning passions of a love greater than he can handle, and spurned by his adored, will as soon set fire to her house, to get her attention.

He'll serenade his darling, promise her the moon, stars, the sun, and even go as far as to push her trolley around the supermarket, but as with ANY Celt, never believe a word they say, and especially the Irish. When under the spell of lust or passion, you takes your choice, they get so carried away, that for the safety of the general public, they really should be put under lock 'n key.

Master of the blarney, the Irish Celt too, has the gift of speech. Peter O'Toole – Terry Wogan, are but just two exam-ples of men gifted with, looks, charm, and so much blarney, that millions turn on the T.V. every Monday/Wednesday/Fri-day, to get their regular dose of the Wogan brand of schmaltz. If Peter O'Toole, was competing on the other side, the females in the U.K. would split down the middle – conquered, by charm and blarney, the downfall of 'many a daycent woman.'

Totally unreliable, heaven help you, if you are ever unfortu-nate enough to have to turn to this volatile creature for help, especially in a time of distress. Don't misunderstand me. His heart, bigger than a mountain, will want to do everything in his power, but the will-power of an Irishman, is the lowest on the totem-pole.

The unpredictability of the Irishman beggars all description, many believe it is fantasy, but I hasten to add, alas! only too true.

A typical example.

Paddy Behan, was walking past a small house, on his way to the village, when he heard someone calling. Turn-ing in the direction, a worried man rushed out shouting, 'for pity's sake, will ye not go straight to the mid-wife, she lives just ten minutes away, my wife's in labour . . . for pity's sake run man!' the distraught man pleaded with him.

Paddy ran, 'I'll not be a moment, just you tell your good woman to hang on,' he rushed, his legs carrying him at a good pace. On the corner of the village he met his old friend Sean Murphy, they got to talking, and soon headed for the pub, the mid-wife and his mission, quite forgotten.

It was 3 months later, that Paddy remembered the mid-wife. Thinking to put matters right, he knocked on the door of the small house, the mother herself opened the door, smiling, Paddy introduced himself and said, 'I was wantin' to know if the bairn had arrived?' The woman gave him a frosty smile, 'And isn't that a kindly thought, 'tis himself asking if the bairn has arrived.'

Then giving him a look that would have nailed him clean to a tree, had she had a gun, she said, 'The baby arrived, it has been christened, and if ye wait a little longer, she'll be going to school soon, but I have a present for ye . . .' She went into the house, returned with a bucket of water, and threw it over him, 'A happy New Year, to you too!'

It's a different story altogether, when Paddy goes courting. He's all attention to his true love's smallest wish, he's at her side, morning, noon, and through the night, given the chance.

Eating is unimportant. Drinking? For sure a man has to keep up his strength. He'll not pay proper attention to his work. He will send you poems, verses of such beauty, that you will be pleasantly surprised, that is, if you are not acquainted with Shelley or Keats. 'Borrowing' is the term Paddy calls it, where's the harm done anyway?

His wit will blind you, and he uses it to lull you into a false sense of security.

'My brother Shamus has produced the latest Irish invention. A parachute that opens on impact.'

OR

Q: How do you stop moles digging up your garden?
A: Hide the spade.

Watch his hands when he tells funny stories, especially if you are in a dimly lit pub, or disco.

34

The Irish Celt is divided in two sections also. The ordinary fellow, who will give you all, money no object, he'll borrow from his grey-haired mother and spend her pension, just to prove it.

Then, you have the sophisticated Dubliner, or the Belfast chap. Travelled, smooth, this type you've really got to watch out for, the imagination of the Irish Romeo works overtime. That lilting accent, the blarney, if you haven't been romanced by an Irishman in love – 'Girl, you ain't seen nothing yet.'

'We've all seen Terry Wogan on the telly, so you have some idea of the charm, these Celts use upon their victims. Just imagine all that charm focused upon you, in a romantic setting, and you have some idea of the danger you are exposed to, it takes tremendous will-power to resist them.

Your Irish smoothie knows all the short-cuts. After wooing you in Ireland, or England, wherever, and getting nowhere, he will then suggest a holiday abroad, a weekend in Paris, or a four-day trip to Norway, he knows a chap in the travel business, no problem, he won't hear of you paying anything, but you insist on separate rooms, if you go along with this venture.

He thinks, ah ha, at last. The sea, the big organge moon, palm trees, it's the perfect setting all right, you stroll by the moonlit shore, it's a night made for love, then you remember what your dear old Mam said before leaving. 'I fell for one night of love, me darlin', and look what happened, it turned into Mick O'Hara, that drunken bum, sitting outside the pub, with his mates . . .'

Hardened by your mother's wise words, you return to the hotel, and he leaves you alone on the first night.

'You've anticipated all problems, and have an ace up your sleeve, all's fair in love and war – right? The second night for him is the Big night, but surprise, surprise, who should arrive at the hotel, but dear old Mam, hungry and ready for a good meal.

Mam enjoys two days, then a telegram arrives, saying your Dad is desperately ill with a severe case of gumboils, so you pack your bags, and rush to the airport, looking great with your newly acquired suntan, but regret in your eyes that your dear romeo, has to stay on alone.

He'll nash his teeth, swear he'll never see you again, but, a man who has had his heart stolen, always comes back to try and retrieve it.

An Irishman is never, ever, to be believed or trusted. He

lives so close to fantasy-land, that anything he dreams up that suits the moment, the situation is, OK.

If you challenge him about the accuracy, or even accuse him of telling outright lies, he'll just say, 'Ach, but you see the little people, 'twas themselves, that told me so . . .' you get nowhere. They'll change any event, any story, and are so convincing, that when you depart from their company, you'll question your own sanity, such is the impact these mercurial creatures have upon others. They see things differently from the rest of us.

Here's an example:

In Eire, the roads are narrow, and not too much traffic about, so it's possible to get up speed, and travel fast. One day, a man in a Jaguar was driving in the country, really going some as he was in a hurry. He saw a straight stretch and put his foot down flat on the accelerator. Up it crept – 55 – 65 – 75.

Then, to his horror, he saw coming out of a field on his left, an enormous load of hay, drawn by a very slow tractor, with two men on it.

There was no way he could stop in time, he was going much too fast, then at the last minute, he wrenched the wheel round, bumped into and over the verge, careered all over the field, desperately fighting to control the car. Round the hayload, bumping, bumping, on to the road once again finally breathing a sigh of relief, getting his wind back.

The two Irishmen on the tractor watched all this open-mouthed. Pat looked at Mick and said, 'Sure 'tis by the grace of God himself Mick, we got out of that field in time.'

It isn't courage you need if you get involved with an Irishman. You need all the luck, a huge shamrock, an avenging angel, and if possible, a good close contact, with Our Heavenly Father, only then will you be able to cope with this Celtic charmer.

But, once the magic, the thrill of the pursuit is over, you'll land down on earth with a bump. He's completely totally committed to the 'Male-is-Boss' syndrome, like his other Celtic brother chauvinism, is his creed also, 'a daycent woman will look to her man first, herself second!'

A Scottish girl, was wooed, and wed her Irish charmer. After two years, the honeymoon was well and truly over. He spent every penny, on drink, whatever. She, cautious by nature, tried to change his ways. The arguments, were fierce and frequent, she flinging accusations at him, of being an 'Irish tinker, a drinker' – he retaliated with a 'miserly, penny pinching Scotch'.

Attending a friend's funeral one day, after another fierce argument, the two of them were leaving the cemetery, to get to the car. Paddy stopped and read the words engraved on an old tombstone.

'Here lies, McGregor, an Engineer, and a pious man.'
'And isn't that just like the Scots' he said turning to his wife,'
'Three men buried in one grave!'

If you've already fallen for an Irish charmer there is nothing on this earth, that can honestly help you, you could look around for a local witch-doctor, and get a potion, which just could break the spell, but while it lasts, no outside help can reach you.

If you are merely playing around or 'thinking' about being serious, a word of advice. Get out while the going is good – don't look back – just go, in any direction, but – away, as far as you can.

✶ ✶ ✶ ✶ ✶ ✶ ✶ ✶ ✶ ✶

The Irish are on a different wave-length to the rest of us.

Two Irishmen are having difficulty getting a lift, so they go their different ways.

One fell over and died of a stroke, but the other one got a lift in a Rolls-Royce, of all things. Soon he began talking to the owner, and to his surprise, he too said he had been hitch-hiking a lift, when a Rolls-Royce pulled up and a luscious blonde told him to get in. She drove him down the road, turned off down a lane, then into a quiet secluded copse. Grabbing hold of the man's hand, she then dragged him deeper and deeper into the woods, laid down, took off her knickers and said, 'You can have anything you want,' 'So I took the Rolls-Royce,' 'You did the right thing' said the tramp, 'her knickers wouldn't have fitted you anyway.'

⊙ ⊙ ⊙ ⊙ ⊙ ⊙ ⊙ ⊙ ⊙ ⊙

The Scotsman

The Scot is akin to his Celtic brothers in many ways. They all share a dislike for the 'SASSENECH' across the border. They also have in their Gaelic make-up much of the fire and passion of the Celt, but the Scot is far more cautious in his approach in wooing the fair sex.

The courtship of a lassie is never the lighthearted affair of his Celtic cousin. Where Paddy or Taffy will fling himself with abandon, heart, body and soul and often his insurance policy, the true Scot, the Gaelic man, unless it's a matter of death or sometimes life, he'll not spend a penny, without considering all the possibilities, or he is guaranteed a good return for his investment.

It goes against the natureof the Scot to be reckless, his canny nature forbids such excesses.

Just occasionally, rarely would be the proper word, a Scot has been known to court a maiden and generously too. There is the tale often told of Ian McGregor, a tall well-built handsome man (rumour had it there was a wee drap of Irish in his blood), who paid in full for his darlin's engagement ring and placed it tenderly upon her finger. He also drew up an insurance policy the day before giving his intended the ring.

The policy covered not only every aspect of her health, her untimely death, but in the case of insanity in the family, or a serious disagreement, resulting in the termination of their betrothal, the ring along with the plush blue velvet box was to be returned immediately.

Despite all these precautions, McGregor was promptly banished from Scotland. This happened, it's true, at the turn of the century, he was escorted to the border, with orders not to set foot in Scotland, until the day before he was to be wed. This precaution was to prevent any other foolish Scot from following his example and giving an expensive gift to a female before they wed. One extravagant gesture like that could cause untold damage to cautious Scotsmen, who had trained their women-folk not to expect anything more than a bunch of daisies, until that day when a Scot committed his hand – seriously in marriage.

For all that, Jock is an ardent wooer, manly, his passion when aroused frightening. One of the world's real he-men is that attractive Scot, Sean Connery, and what woman in her right mind could resist the charm of Sean, if he put his mind to go a-wooing?

Make no mistake, the man in the kilt can be verra romantic, passionate, charming, even if he does keep his hand on his sporran – where his money is – when he declared undying love for the object of his affection.

There's no sweeping a Scot off his feet, but once his heart is entangled, watch out, he can be dangerous. But kindly too.

McPherson was taking his fiancee for a drive on a lovely summer's evening. They drove past the shopping centre, passed a popcorn stand. 'Wow!' said Moira, 'That popcorn smells good, really yummy.' 'Ach, Lassie,' said McPherson, generously, 'I'll drive a wee bit closer, so you can get a better whiff of it.'

Careful! that's Jock.

But if any of you young ladies are emotionally interested in a Scot, dismiss that unkind rumour that he keeps his sporran on while making love – courting. Check any J. Bond film and you'll see that Sean Connery has nothing on but his tartan shorts!

A question which comes around as often as Christmas is, DO they wear anything under their kilt? I am honour bound not to answer this question, but I will tell you about Sandy McInley, who was courting Maggie Murphy. Sandy was reserved, a quiet fellow, Maggie was fun-loving, lively, smiling, mischievous, and she kept on, and on, asking Sandy – on the odd occasion when he wore it – whether he had anything under his kilt.

One Saturday night, Sandy had had enough! Wearing his kilt especially for the evening, they went dancing, then afterwards had a quiet drink at a corner table of their local.

Several drinks later Maggie started, did he or didn't he have anything underneath. Sandy excused himself, went to the Gents then returned. 'You've been after me to tell you whether I have or haven't, Maggie. So why don't you put your hand up my kilt and find out for yourself.' Maggie looked amazed, she knew how shy Sandy was and couldn't believe her ears. 'You mean it,

Sandy?' He nodded his head. Discreetly she gently slid her hand up his leg, up to his thigh, then let out a shriek, quickly she withdrew her hand, her forefinger was caught in a small mouse-trap.

She's none the wiser!
They have a great sense of humour in every way, but they don't laugh about money. It's not that they won't spend it, they will – eventually. Ingrained since birth, born bred to respect this valuable acquisition, they hate to part with it, well not too much at a time anyway. It's a national disease, they can't help it.

Hewan McCann's young lady mentioned that her birthday was coming up soon and Hewan thought and thought, and thought, but he just couldn't think of an inexpensive present.

His mother had just finished making him a pair of tartan breeches to go with his best Sunday kilt. She casually remarked that there was a yard of material left and no doubt his clever Jeannie could make something out of it.

Hewan was delighted, a present and it hadn't cost him a penny. Next weekend he took his girl-friend high up on the heath. On top he spun around fast on his heels, his kilt flying as he twirled.

'Jeannie, did ye see anything, lassie?'
She blushed, said she had not, so Hewan spun around again, a second time, until his kilt was horizontal, blissfully unaware that he had forgotten to put his breeches on.

'Surely, Jeannie, ye saw it this time?'
'Aye,' blushing still . . . 'I'm . . . I'm sure I did.'
'Well, I'd hoped you'd like it, cos' you're getting three feet of it for your birthday next week . . .'

The Scot is a male chauvinist, aggressive, in charge dominant. He sees himself as the Caveman bringing home the carcass, the female always attending to his needs.

Even the most cultured Scotsman and you've got your lout, your slob, in Scotland, just as in other countries – even the most refined Scot, deep down inside, believes that the female was intended by nature to walk behind a man and appreciate the importance of being his chosen mate.

Outwardly he'll try and conform to the changing times, but

41

it's very hard for a Scot to ever think of a female as equal in brains or ability.

Whatever his shortcomings, he'll respond to a pretty face with all the alacrity of his fellow Celt, relishes a chase, indeed thrives on it.

FACTS ABOUT THE SCOT

His weakness is his ego. It's colossal: Drink, loves the booze, but many can keep it under control.
Loves sport, Good Food, His woman under control.

* * * * * * * * * *

You must play a very careful game with your Jock. The sophisticated type are always the ones to be most on guard about. He's not careless, reckless, like Taff or Paddy. If you want to get him to the altar, he'll want you untarnished, with the label upon you – 'Untouched by human hands – a virgin. He wants value for his money.

Like every man, the Gaelic likes a challenge and does his utmost to seduce you, it's all part of his game. You've got a few things going for you, and as they say about Royalty, same thing applies to Scotsmen. When you come into contact, use flattery, not skillfully, but by the shovelful, they love it. Admire everything about him, even his breathing, he will think you the greatest event since the creation of the zip fastner.

A tactic used by Jock, to good effect, is an old and tried one. After several outings, the disco, the cinema, the darts match, Jock's blood pressure will be mounting, reaching combustion point probably and he might give you an ultimatum. Surrender or lose your laird!

Don't fall for it! Say anything, but say NO!

He'll stay away, play hard to get, all the old, tried and tested games that lovers play. Hold fast. Don't ring him. He'll go boozing with his mates, try and chat up other dolly-birds, it's all a waiting game. If you give in you've lost. Then he'll just happen to be at the local and see you, now he makes his move. Bear one thing in mind, if he's lasted all the months you were together, used after-shave, trimmed his moustache, you just must know you're special.

After he 'accidentally' meets you in the pub and resumes courtship, you'll have to decide quickly 'To be or not to Be'.

Once back in harness let him play his natural chauvinistic

role. Let him strut, preen, boast or brag, give him space. In no way hint he came after you. That he won't stomach, he wants his pride, must have it, so give it to him.

Be feminine. Wear lots of perfume and above all arrange a special dinner for him at your home. Don't let your mother argue you out of it. Get her to take a weekend in Seville, so you have the house to yourself. If she hasn't the money, or dislikes foreign travel, pack her off for a two-day tour of Colwyn Bay, in North Wales, that's far enough. In the winter, with snow on the ground, there's no shortage of seats on the charabanc. Make sure she takes your Dad with her.

Make sure they've got sandwiches and a flask of tea and a packet of eccles cakes, in case they get homesick! A map just in case the bus breaks down and have to hitch-hike home; be quite ruthless about this, it's no time to get sentimental!

Very Important!

All this must be arranged before a big match. A rugby special or a soccer high spot. Bribe, threaten, do anything, but get a couple of good seats, the best. Give them to him over a quiet meal and accompany him to the football. Now you've really gone up in his estimation. But – more is to follow.

Before the big afternoon outing, prepare everything he likes to eat, all his favourite dishes and a stack of beer, some wine for yourself. Now, with Mum 'n Dad rattling along in a charabanc, somewhere along the wild west coast of Wales or careering over the Severn Bridge, you prepare yourself for a cosy evening with just one reservation.

Jock must think, be led to think, that Mam is enjoying a late bingo session and dear old Dad, nursing a sick pigeon, down on the allotment where he keeps them. Just in case your kilted beau wants to play housey-housey! By the time the two tourists return from their winter vacation in Wales, you should be happily engaged and planning to name the date.

It's all a question of strategy.

*

A Scotsman, a devout, pious man, who had given years of service to his church, fell upon hard times. As he was saying his prayers one night, he beseeched God to let him win the football pools, a big decent win to see him through his old age – in exchange for his years of devout service.

The next week, once again, the same prayer. Nothing

happened, no envelope with the cheque. Again he pleaded his cause. Still, no answer. God was silent. After a month, the Scot fell upon his knees complaining, 'Why, dear lord, don't you give me a break, just once, I'll not ask again!'

Suddenly the voice of the Almighty was heard: 'How about giving ME a break? At least fill in a coupon!'

A Scot was engaged in a fierce argument with a bus conductor, as to whether the fare was 9p or 10p. In a fit of rage the conductor picked up the Scot's suitcase and flung it off the bus into the river. It sank with a splash. 'Enough,' said the Scot, 'you've gone too far noo. First yee try tae rob me, and then yee droon ma wee laddie.'

◉ ◉ ◉ ◉ ◉ ◉ ◉ ◉ ◉ ◉ ◉

Northerners

The Northern Englishman, is as different from his Southern counterpart as melon is to mustard.

In habits, outlook, behaviour pattern, he has far more in common with his Scot or Celtic neighbour.

Completely chauvinistic, his attitude towards the fair sex dates back to the caveman, and he sees no point in changing it. He has none of the smooth, polished, sophisticated approach of the Southerner, in particular the London chap. What's more wouldn't be caught dead using such sissified manners.

Shrewd, tough in business, he'll horse-trade with the best. Blunt, rough often in manner, he doesn't mind getting his hands dirty. 'Where there's muck, there's brass' has been his slogan for years, decades.

He enjoys female company, unlike the Aussie, thinks a woman should be decorative, useful, if necessary, but never equal in the brain department, furthermore sees no point in changing the status quo.

Like most British men, he will publicly support women's rights, he'll encourage his wife, daughter, to enroll for classes on 'How to become Prime Minister', then make damn sure that neither are given the chance opportunity, by voting for a Bill which is against such nonsense.

It's not that he's dishonest, it's the way he thinks, the way he's been brought up, indeed the way all men in their right minds should think. He firmly believes and practises that good old saying, 'let 'em – women – have a bit of harmless fun, but make sure they don't have any real weapons to play with'.

If you are contemplating living in the North take heed, it's man's territory, and you'll not change it.

Your Northerner likes to think of himself as 'down to earth', doesn't go for that 'fancy stuff', but nevertheless demands all the luxuries, surroundings, the frills and attention, his Southern cousin enjoys in the big city.

He'll never admit it, 'it's not manly, lad', but he enjoys the polish, the continental cuisine, imported wines, but passes off this indulgence as 'pleasing the little woman', like most men he's a hypocrite at heart.

45

Sport is king up North. With many it's a way of life, it's their religion. Soccer to some northerners is the closest thing to total happiness. This true story illustrates it perfectly.

A wife petitioned for divorce, the judge asked her for an example of her husband's bad behaviour. She replied, 'Last year Harry asked me if I had anything to say before the Soccer season started.'
Divorce granted

Greyhounds – Horse-racing – Snooker – Boxing, Northerners love to gamble, they are loyal beyond the call of duty. Fanatics, which leaves a girl very much on the side lines, for she really has to compete to get any attention.

Hobbies have broken more marriages up North than infidelity. After a romantic courtship, a young couple got married, and settled down to domestic bliss, or so the young bride thought. Before the end of the year, the marriage was almost over.

Brian was a pigeon fancier, and, a small-time breeder – part-time anyway. His whole time away from his regular job was the pigeons. He bought them special food, watched their diet, an occasional pedigree bird, he raced them, talked to them, spent more time chatting up the feathered birds, bottom of the garden in their coop, than he did his real bird in the house.

Sue his wife pleaded, coaxed, threatened, begged him just once a week, could they go out and meet people, relax over a drink. He promised, of course, and always made an excuse.

She told him the pigeons were wrecking their marriage, but no use. She sued for divorce, saying the birds got more attention than she did. He didn't bother to contest it, it was true.

If you are hopelessly bewitched by a Northerner, if you will sit dutifully, patiently listening to your man, expound upon politics, party-line, or foreigners and the rest, you'll fit in nicely into Northern surroundings.

As men go, some of them can be very generous, especially when moved by guilt or conscience. He occasionally spoils his female, gets sentimental if he remembers about birthdays, or an anniversary, but don't let this fool you. He's a hard man to handle, he's just got to be boss. If you can't accept that you're in real trouble; if you can, you haven't any big problems, but on the other hand, who wants to be a second-rate citizen?

Like all men, when he's pursuing his female, he'll do his best to get a 'trial run', so this is the time to trot out your relatives, the male ones. It's standard practise in Spain, Greece

47

or Italy to trot out the men of the family, as a kind of subtle warning to the suitor, not to try any funny business. If you are short of males, ring up Equity, and train a couple of actors to behave like relatives, it can do wonders for your image.

Learn all you can about sport, any sport. Pigeons Horses Greyhounds, you never know when you'll need this information. It takes guts. Personally I can't stand greyhounds, lean, lanky, unfed looking, even when they have feasted, a ratty looking animal, no thank you. But, love conquers all, and Northerners go OTT, right over the top regarding their sport, it's true too, about 'love me, love my dog'.

Olive married her fellow with the full knowledge that he was a greyhound man, he raced them, and made a bit of money. Playing the part of a dutiful wife, she groomed the dog, exercised him, fed him, watched his diet, and was a 100% perfect partner. Nights were spent at tracks, at meetings, she didn't complain.

One bitterly cold night, the night before a big race, that was the night it happened, the straw that broke the camel's back. 'Caesar', their racing dog, was entered for a big race the following night. On this very cold night, her husband Stan brought the dog into the house, upstairs, and then suggested to his wife that she sleep on the settee, and 'Caesar' sleep in the big bed with him – just for that one night. She couldn't believe her ears; he insisted, so did she, he then told her she'd have to share the bed with both of them.

She packed her things, took the youngster, and went home to mother. Northerners don't fool around when it comes to hobbies.

Your question will be. Are they all mad about pigeons and greyhounds up north? No! certainly not. Some of them favour ferrets, fighting cocks, and bantams.

He likes going out, your north country type. The Clubs there are some of the best in the U.K. Plenty of good food, good company, booze, and down to earth jokes, none of your London humour thanks very much. Here's an example.

'Doc,' Mr Clyde pleaded, 'you've got to help me.'
'What's the trouble?'
'Listen, Doc, you see my hair, it's black, right?'
'Yes . . .'
'Now my wife has black hair, but she gave birth to a red-headed baby, what do you think, Doc?'

48

'How often do you have sex – three times a week?' the doctor asked.

Mr Clyde shook his head.

'Once a week?'

Mr Clyde shook his head

'Once a month?'

Again he shook his head.

'Once every six months?'

'No,' said Clyde.

'Once a year?' the doctor asked.

'Just about,' said Clyde.

'Ah well,' the doctor patted him on the back, 'that explains it, you're just a bit rusty.'

If you decide a Northerner is for you, best of British anyway; a word of advice. If you should find a ferret or a greyhound in your bed, don't stand for any nonsense, do what the cave-women did when wolves came creeping around to share their cave, give it a quick swift kick, up the khyber pass. This is 1986, and women do have a few, just a few, rights!

⊚ ⊚ ⊚ ⊚ ⊚ ⊚ ⊚ ⊚ ⊚ ⊚ ⊚

Southerners

The archetypal Englishman, as portrayed by Cary Grant, Rex Harrison, Edward Fox, is not a true picture of the millions of males who live in England. The men from the North, Devon men, Yorkshire, Lancashire men, men from all parts of the Kingdom, but it is the old school type kind, that people abroad, immediately think of, when an Englishman is mentioned.

Disliked by his fellow Brit, Jock, Taffy and Paddy, our St George differs too in temperament, outlook and manner. Trained from years at 'prep school', public schools and either Oxford/Cambridge, he remains a bit of an enigma, not understood and certainly not trusted by many.

His cool, casual manner often conceals burning emotions. One girl described him as 'like a volcano, simmering on the outside, but a roaring fire deep inside'.

St George hates to get excited about anything, he finds any sort of emotion rather wearying and, dash it, all in bad taste, it really dates back to Sir Francis Drake, if not before.

Sir Francis, as history tells us, was enjoying a game of bowls, when his lookout reported the hated enemy, the Spanish Navy, steaming up the English Channel, the officer awaited instructions.

Sir Francis gazed calmly seawards, then said, 'We shall conclude our game, when it is finished, we'll give those foreigners the thrashing of their life.'

And they did!

That kind of cool, detached attitude, sums up your Englishman, and has helped many a 'limey' through difficult situations, crisis and, indeed, stands him in good stead. Emotion, getting all het up, is for foreigners and women. Any man worth his salt tackles a tough situation calmly, methodically, quietly.

Can you wonder that Jock, Taffy and Paddy want to flatten him sometimes?

Now don't be misled, the Englishman can be a tiger, passionate without any sort of reservation. But – his passion is

51

only for two things. Cricket and rugby! he really lets himself go when he watches either of these two great sports.

Foreigners are low on the totem pole. St George looks with disdain upon anything foreign. He avoids all foreign food, if possible, having tried it once, when travelling overseas he has discovered he prefers his native food and sticks to that. Roast beef, Yorkshire pudding and all the trimmings, however, he has been known to sneak off for a quick Tandoori curry, when the local 'fish 'n chip' shop is shut.

Foreign sports are shrugged off as sports for foreigners. He is incredibly brave, quite fearless in action. His feats of courage are legion. One brief incident will give you a graphic picture of how an Englishman handled himself, when in grave peril.

Cary Grant was trapped in a Fortress just on the edge of the Kalahari Desert. Alone with no hope of help in sight, 10,000 natives brandishing cutlasses, swords, their evil faces bent on revenge. They stormed the Fortress, looking for the English enemy. Hidden by a high wall, Cary knew it was just a matter of minutes before they discovered him and put him to death.

Stepping out from behind the pillar, brandishing his revolver, unflinching, fearless and brave, Cary shouted, 'Hands up, you are all under arrest,' so stunned were the natives by this act of bravery/audacity, they surrendered.

They just don't give up, it's the same thing, courting a girl, it's a game, often of bluff. A girl I know tried every which way to avoid going to her chap's apartment for drinks, she couldn't think of any way to refuse without hurting his feelings, yet she was only too aware of what he had on his mind. Then she came up with a brilliant idea. She bought a can of 'Fly Spray' and put it in her handbag! It worked.

Englishmen have a great sense of humour, they relish the bawdy type of humour which flourished during the Music Hall days, no prude is your old school tie chap. Romantic too. He'll carry a bunch of flowers for his love and be damned to the world, not so your Welsh man, your Scot or Irish, fear of being laughed at by their mates, doesn't bother your English suitor, he revels in doing unexpectedly foolish or plain daft things, all in the name of love.

During the last war, a dashing airman, very much taken by the charms of a young actress, won a rooster at an auction and promptly arrived at a Mayfair block of flats, where the young actress lived and gallantly with a bow, presented her with his choice offering. The rooster had to stay in a closet all night. When a woman tenant protested next morning to the janitor, that she heard a rooster crowing all through the night, she was dismissed as having the usual deliriums.

Trapping an Englishman, if you are serious, must be done with finesse and style. He adores a pretty girl, but, abhors anything too flashy, at least for a permanent arrangement. He'll promise, the earth too, why not, and run away when his independence is threatened.

He admires anyone who 'plays it cool', it's his own style, the obvious puts him right off, so there you have a clue to his nature. Let him do the chasing, like any real man, he wants to pursue, so let him. Send him funny verses. One chap was so amused, at first, then charmed, by his girl's orginality, she finally got him to the altar. Here's one that appealed to him.

Under the spreading Chestnut bough
There sat a young milkmaid milking a cow
Along came the farmer and gave her the sack.
So she turned the cow over and poured the milk back.

or

They sat upon a grassy bank,
And she was all a-quiver,
He undid her suspender belt,
And her leg fell in the river.

* * * * * * * * * *

The wry sense of humour, attributed to our St George, is very much part of his character.

A difficult lady, spending time with her daughter and English son-in-law, was reading the papers on Sunday afternoon. She called to her son-in-law, working in his study, and requested he turn down the air-conditioning. He did and returned to his study.

Five minutes later, fanning herself, she called for him to kindly turn it up again. Five minutes later, another shout, this went on for well over an hour.

His wife, in their bedroom, asked him in a whisper, 'Geoffrey, why are you playing such a silly game?' He smiled, 'I'm driving her mad, or I will, when she finds out we haven't got air-conditioning.'

Gallantry is part of his nature, much as he hates any kind of public emotion, our St George hates to see a women cry and will do anything to help. Such an occasion rose when travelling through Australia.

It was a hot day, one of those baking Australian days, when everyone has a perpetual thirst.

Seated in one compartment was a young mother, nursing her new-born baby. Opposite her was a drunken, uncouth man, smelling of whisky, when the train stopped at his station, the drunkard stood up, swaying on his feet, he peered at the baba, and said 'That's the ugliest baby I ever saw in my life.' He stumbled off, leaving the young mother in a flood of tears.

The train started up again, an Englishman was making his way along the corridor, to the refreshment bar, and he heard and saw the sobbing young woman. Moved by such a sight he opened her compartment door, enquiring 'was there anything at all he could do to help?'

The mother shook her head, tears streaming down her face, between sobs she said, 'A . . . man . . . a very rude man . . . he was dreadful, said the rudest things . . .'

'There, there,' said our hero, 'it's not worth getting yourself all upset about, tell you what, it's such a hot day, I'll get you a nice cold drink. How about that?' Nodding her head, the young mother still crying, thanked him.

Five minutes later, St George returned, with an ice-cold orange drink and handed it to her. 'Now drink that, you'll feel much better, and look, I've brought a banana for the monkey.'

The Southern Englishman has no hang-ups about women. None of the chauvinistic outlook that marks his neighbours.

He takes females in his stride, nonchalant, casual, he doesn't see what all the fuss is about 'Man's rights', unless of course you are talking about Lord's Cricket Club, or the Oval, man's domain, that sort of stuff, then you are on dangerous ground.

For the wealthier type, his Club in St James, is his refuge too, but taken by large, the Englishman is very happy to have the 'little woman' around, or to watch the prettiest sight in town. Chorus girls kicking up their legs! Dashed good fun, good sport . . . You could do worse than commit yourself to this type.

◎ ◎ ◎ ◎ ◎ ◎ ◎ ◎ ◎ ◎

Other Types

Americans

American men are outgoing, gregarious, uninhibited, and chase a 'dame' with enthusiasm, and gusto.

They have none of the devious sophisitication of the Englishman, the blarney of the Irishman, the chauvinistic approach of the Welshman or Northerner, or the plain unromantic approach of the Scot.

Americans enjoy the company of the fair sex more than any other race of man, they are the complete antithesis of the Australian male.

He loves to surprise his lady love, with unexpected gifts, taking her out, he openly shows his affection, or lust, and bedding a wench is as much a part of the American scene, as Mom's apple pie. They differ only in accents.

The Southerners like to think, they are far more courteous, than the New Yorker, not so. The New Englander – (Bostonian) is more reserved, (pure fiction). The Texan is always larger than life, especially travelling overseas, and your Carolina beau, is very, very, smooth indeed.

Spoiling the female is tradition in America, its part 'n parcel, of the way every healthy American boy is brought up. They have regard and respect for the female brain too, an attribute sadly lacking in chauvinistic Britain, no matter what our local politicians say – same thing for Europeans.

Americans are equal. There is no class hang-up in the States. Every male knows he has a chance to make it to the White House. Every female knows, she can marry a prince and live happily ever after. The classless accent, makes it possible for the elevator operator to sit down in a restaurant with the President of a company, with no embarrassment, no sense of being unequal. Each to his own pursuit, one guy makes it to the top of the heap, the other doesn't. His attitude is, it's no big deal, life goes on, don't it?

This same attitude applies when chasing his 'doll'. I'm a fella, you're a dame let's make pretty music together.

Your Yank spends whatever he's got – sure you've got the penny-pinchers, but speaking generally – they are generous. If he's from the South he'll call his girl, his 'sugar', 'Honey', his 'baby-doll'. If he's from Brooklyn or New York, she's his 'Broad', 'Chick' or 'Dame'.

Dining out, it's the lady who calls the shots. Whatever baby wants, she's sure gonna get, or, the next best thing. You like gambling, then head for the Casino. Disco O.K., let's make music, if you fancy more high class stuff, like a Broadway, West End show, no problem, your Yankee Doodle Dandy aims to please, all the way.

He'll bring flowers when calling, scanning the apartment for the location of the bedroom, as he presents a bouquet to you. Don't be deceived by the boyish charm, it's all part of an act, he's as much a predator as his Brit brothers.

He's a very difficult adversary to handle, your American pursuer. He's so open, genuinely anxious to please, with no apparent guile, that saying 'no' to one of them, is almost like refusing to give candy to a child.

He's not into any long term commitments, and especially if he's overseas, say the U.K. long courtships are out, they look for a quick return for their investment in a broad: flowers, dining-wining, then it's let's get together baby. If some action isn't forthcoming, they move on to fresh pastures, or, put it this way. Your visiting Yank likes company when he's saying his prayers at night.

Our American cousins are only here for a short stay. A year, maybe two year period, then they move on, so to get serious about one of our old ex-colonialists, is really not too wise.

The Americans claimed massive victories here, during the last war, and although they come over in smaller numbers, they still collect scalps, so question No. 1 is: Now to handle these dashing New World warriors?

Not easily, you've got a better chance if you live out of London. The attractions aren't so varied, or limited, and if you are good company, pretty, he's not going to lose you too soon.

Take him home to meet the family, tell him it's a 'hands across the sea' gesture. Make sure your Gran is around, she'll regale him with stories about the last war, the tricks the Yanks got up to, and the brides who were so shamefully deceived. By the time the visit is over, making sure he's had a splendid English high tea, his behaviour will be above reproach, he'll keep his hands in his pants pocket – it won't last, but it will give you time to re-think your strategy.

Some of the stories our cousins, spun to our ingenuous war bridges makes the mind boggle, so don't believe half of what the son of G.I. Joe says. Hundreds, no thousands of blushing

British brides sailed away to the New World, many of them in no doubt the Hollywood ending awaiting them in the Land of opportunity.

One bride married a Texan. His little 'old Daddy had a chain of stores, a ranch, so many employees, why life was just a ball. When she eventually got to the outskirts of Houston she discovered the 'chain' was just two links. A general store, with a gas-station, right next to it. A couple of black fellows worked the pumps, and guess who was Daddy's assistant in the general store? Right! our hero from the wars, G.I. Joe.

But that was one of the kinder, gentler, little jokes played on our naive British brides. One or two of them had real shocks.

One girl married a black soldier, her destination after docking at New York, was Georgia, the deep South, where she would live in a big house, like the one in 'Gone with the Wind', servants, horses, acres of land.

She arrived, to find a shack, outdoor plumbing, one water faucet (tap) and a bedroom, with a leaky corrugated tin roof. She didn't bother to unpack, just turned around, and made her way to the ship and Britain. No girl ever appreciated the modest council house of her parents' more.

The Texans, are never able to resist the 'Evverthin' is bigger 'n better in Texas' so a word when dating your Yank. Take anything he says with a huge pinch of salt, they don't mean to brag, it's natural as breathing, no harm meant.

Chuck was really out to impress Lily, he told her about his family, all cowboys, from way back.

My Cowboy pappy walked into a saloon and ordered a glass of whisky. Just as he was about to take his first sip, a fly landed on the bar, next to his glass. When the fly took off, he spat at it, and the direct hit brought it tumbling to the floor, but the fly survived and flew off.

'That sure was a mighty accurate shot,' said the bartender. 'Ain't nothing,' growled the cowboy, 'you should see my 'ole pappy.' The following evening he brought his father into the same saloon, and ordered two whiskeys. As they were about the drink, a fly flew past and the father brought it to the floor mortally wounded.

'That was incredible,' said the astonished barman.

'My 'ole pappy's even better,' said the father. A few days later all three strolled in and ordered drinks. This time the fly didn't appear for a while, but as soon as it did, the old man spat powerfully at the insect. The fly just wavered mid-flight, made a peculiar noise, then flew off.

'That was no-where near as good,' said the bartender.

'Even so,' said the old man, 'that one'll never breed again.'

Impressed Lily asked chuck if this really happened, he assured her it was plain nothing just Texas style 'living'. When Lil asked him to drop her off at Buckingham Palace, and said 'goodnight,' he looked at her in stunned amazement. 'Say, do you REALLY live here.' She smiled back, and said it was nothing, just London style 'living!

Your best weapon against a healthy, normal, red-blooded American, is to take a course in Karate, at least physically, you'll be able to handle him, if the situation turns to wrestling.

One of our uniformed, American guests, was arrested recently in a hotel on the South coast. An officer, in the American Forces, he was found completely nude in the lobby, chasing a woman. He was freed at the court-martial, on a mere technicality. It specifically states in the army manual, that an officer need not be in uniform, providing he is properly attired for the sport in which he is engaged.

The American male, believes in mating, he claims regular mating sessions are wholesome, healthy, and good for growth, stimulates the mind, sharpens the appetite, helps to strengthen the bond between the USA and the people of the country, he is currently visiting/working in. If you accept that line of bull, you deserve to be sent to the 'Women's Lib' Disciplinary Committee, for trial.

They behave the same way back home. Chasing women, Yanks think, is the greatest form of sport ever invented, until something else comes along, why change the rules?

A New York recruit was undergoing an oral examination for an appointment to the Police Force, and was asked –

'If your beat was a lonely path in our Central Park, and a beautiful young girl rushed up to you, and declared that a strange man had jumped out of the bushes suddenly and grabbed her and hugged her, and kissed her, and then attacked her, what would you do?'

He replied instantly, 'I'd endeavour to reconstruct the crime.'

Handling a Yank, is like trying to cope with an octopus, but let's face it, some people find that a terrific sport too.

⊙ ⊙ ⊙ ⊙ ⊙ ⊙ ⊙ ⊙ ⊙ ⊙ ⊙

Foreigners

Foreigners are quite different to us, they speak in a foreign tongue, their way of life, behaviour pattern is foreign, and frankly, they take a lot of getting used to.

The accent absolutely gets to some women, it fascinates them, they go overboard in such a big way, that they'll put up with bad breath, dandruff, garlic, hair so oily, that he needs a cape a plastic one to hold the drips. However, all these so small irritations are of no importance, when he opens his mouth to speak, the sheer magic sends some maidens into raptures.

Their approach to the British female is quite unlike anything they get from the local talent. Carlos, Pierre, Wilhelm or Gregos, will bow from the waist, kiss your hand, look lingeringly into your eyes, even if he's holding up traffic, escort a girl across a busy street with so much care and attention. The Queen Mum couldn't have more courtesy or gallantry.

This kind of behaviour is enough to make a strong Aussie keel right over, and the rest of the local lads to eye them very suspiciously.

Foreigners, frequently have impeccable manners, they make the Brits look positively uncouth, which is one reason why there was such strong opposition to joining the Common Market.

They're a mixture of Sacha Distel, Richard Clayderman, Charles Boyer – remember him? and Omar Shariff, and the maidens swoon with delight, or plot to meet such a man.

Unlike the Brit, when his heart is wrapped up in his lady-love, he doesn't care who knows, who sees, where he is, he will stop in Piccadilly and say, 'You are the most beau-i-ful voman in ze world,' he will kiss your hand sending shivers down your spine.

A restaurant, surroundings, mean nothing at all, he's oblivious to people, places. Gazing into your eyes, holding both your hands, making you feel so special. It's a rotten waste of spaghetti bolognaise, but what the heck. He'll go on his knees, just as you've got a mouthful of spaghetti finally and tells you he adores you, worships you, pressing your other hand to his

63

heart, and, if he's bribed the violinist, the music, dead on cue will play, 'Love is a many splendoured thing'.

And this is just for openers, the big scene comes with dinner!

You have a date for dinner. Foreigners are very impatient, don't waste time. You arrange to meet him in town, rather than have him pick you up at home, this is no time to give your zenophobic Dad a heart attack. He'll meet you outside the restaurant, a posy of flowers in his hand, impatiently, pacing up and down.

Sweeping you to a corner table, he pulls out your chair, his eyes caressing every inch of your body, you already feel like you're the main course.

He orders the meal in faultless, French, Spanish and while you are sipping wine, he caresses your hand, turns it over, ah! you think, he'll tell my fortune, but no, he speaks 'Nevaire, in all my travels 'ave I met so wonderful, so perr-rfect, so, so, fas-cin-a-ting a voman . . .' More kisses and burning looks of passion.

All this before, you've touched the soup!

But, it's dinner with Prince Charming himself, all those words you've heard Omar Shariff, Marcel Maestronni, Alain Delon say, all those wonderful words of love, this man is telling you – Susy Blonks, who works for the Gas Company., you want to pinch yourself, to find out whether you're dreaming.

Alas, it's all a trap. Foreigners know all about the sex-starved females of Britain. They've met them in Spain, Majorca, when on holiday. The first glimpse of the sun, they abandon all restraint and behave like a bunch of nymphomaniacs let loose among the Canadian Cavalry.

It's up to you to shatter the picture of Brit girls, being starved for romance. All you have to remember is, most of them are here for a short visit. A student for a season, a temporary job, to learn English, not one of them have any intention of getting serious, and absolutely NO intention of playing housey-housey for real. Your passionate Don Carlos or Luigi, Rofolfo, has more than likely a fiancee back home, filling up her bottom drawer, pouring over her weekly letter from Britain, and counting the days when he'll be back with her.

Foreigners, like MP's mean everything they say, AT THE TIME, but they are never meant to be taken seriously, everyone knows that. Sweet words, flowery words, flattery, compliments, it's part of a game, the language of courting, every wooer, pursuer, every lover's ammunition. The Brit girls used to the caution of their fellow Brits, are overwhelmed by the foreigner who shovels it on so thick, no wonder the naive young maidens fall for this line of old rope.

The Arabs are even worse! when they come here, see our girls in the shortest of shorts, they go bananas! Can you wonder why? Back home, their women are wrapped in black from head to toe. Yashmaks cover their faces, and as for courting. Grandmother, mother, sister, two brothers, all sit around in a circle, when he courts his bride-to-be, so Britain is some kind of free harem.

It's not always the foreigner who is at fault. Everyone must now have heard about the woman in Dallas, who forced her way into Omar Shariff's motel room, and demanded he make love to her at the point of a gun. He stripped, as she demanded, and showed he was unable to perform under such circumstances – no man could.

Not so, according to Dr Philip Sarrel, Director at Yale University, of Human Sexuality. He told in his casebook, how a 30-year-old man was accosted by two women, and forced to make love at gunpoint, to both of them; Dr Sarrel speaking at a Manchester conference said, 'Yes, terror made men able to perform the sex act.'

One of my two scottish fans, Sadie McGoonhan – not her real name – from Sauchiehall St, Glasgow, was so carried away by the article about Dr Sarrel, that she wrote to me.

Sadie is hopelessly romantic. Square shaped, in her 50's, a spinster, she is not physically attractive to her fellow-man. Jock Muldoon put it this way, 'Och aye, if she's the best thing to offer, I'll stick to beer.'

Her letter read,

'For years I've had my heart set on Sandy McGiffey, the butcher. After that piece in the paper, I made up me mind. I went round Friday evening, about closing time, to Sandy's shop. He tried to lock me out, but I wouldna take no for an answer. I locked the door behind me, and tried to terrorize him into making love to me, but he wouldna do so. I was verra, verra patient. So I pushed him into one of those big fridges, to try and get him to change his mind, I only left him in there for ten minutes, just long enough to scare him.

When I dragged him out, he had ice everywhere, his hair was white with frost, he was shivering all over. I was verra put out and disappointed. Please tell me what it is I'm doing wrong?

Sadly disappointed
Sadie.

I wrote and told her, freezing the object of one's affection wasn't likely to get a warm response.

But – back to foreigners!

If you find yourself getting wedding bell sounds in your ears, get Interpol to run a check on him, if he's an Arab, for sure, some of them have three wives. Get hold of your MP and get him to work for you, after all your vote got him his cushy job, make him work for a change.

Bear in mind, although some foreigners speak English, they think in a foreign language, so be very, very, careful with foreigners. Promise everything and give – nothing.

There are only two types of people who can afford to make a mistake only once.

Virgins and Paratroopers.

✷ ✷ ✷ ✷ ✷ ✷ ✷ ✷ ✷ ✷

A Frenchman was on his first trip to London, for an International Trade conference, and decided to brush up on his English pronounciation. Not wishing to make any mistakes, he took the opportunity on the Underground to pore over his little booklet, and in frustration could be heard muttering.

T-H-R-O-U-G-H.   pronounced   throo'
T-R-O-U-G-H   pronounced   troff'
P-L-O-U-G-H   pronounced   pla-ow'
T-H-O-U-G-H   pronounced   thaow'

'Zis language, 'C'est terrible C'est stupide . . .'

Having reached his destination, he boarded the escalating stairs. At the top he was greeted with a large poster proclaiming:

BLACK AND WHITE MINSTRELS PRONOUNCED
SUCCESS.
whereupon he shot himself.

◎ ◎ ◎ ◎ ◎ ◎ ◎ ◎ ◎ ◎

Australian

The Australian male is quite unique, a character living 12,000 miles away from the U.K., and, some say, that's O.K. with most of us.

Tough, hard-drinking, with a chip on his shoulder, where the 'Brit' is concerned – the 'Pommie' as the Aussie chooses to call all British men, he's an individual moulded by the unique environment of a Continent, with so much space, plenty of sun, sheep stations, and miles and miles of land in every direction.

The Aussie likes plenty of action, fast action. Just as Australia is a young country, it's men are also in a heck of a hurry to, 'get there fast', whether it's to pile up the dollars, become the world's best tennis players, or fly to Britain, their motto is, 'let's go'.

Their life-style reflects a lot of American touches. T.V. shows, trendy clothes, sky-scraper hotels. Every new American fashion reaches Australia almost before it gets to Europe. At the race tracks in Sydney, Melbourne, and other cities, you'll find the most elegantly dressed females, they make Ascot look like a second hand shop, they may, distance-wise, be quite a long way from the acknowledged centres of fashion, but there is nothing lacking in the newest technology, fashion, or cars in Aussie-land.

So much for technology, the Australian male however, still remains very dated in his attitude towards the female. A 'Sheila' as he calls his girl, is someone he best enjoys when alone. It's a strange behaviour pattern of the Aussie male, but when in mixed company, the men gravitate towards one end of the room, and the women cluster in groups, the other end. At cocktail parties, any kind of party, this invariably happens, people visiting from other countries find it quite extraordinary.

The Aussie male – with a few exceptions – finds it embarrassing somewhat, to make small talk with a female, when at a gathering, after a period overseas, the rough edges smoothed down, they can be very charming, but the local talents are a very strange breed.

A girl meeting an Aussie in the U.K., might find him rather

different to the average fellow, but for anyone getting serious about the male from 'down under' the information given above can be invaluable.

They like drinking, it's a national pastime, betting, horse-racing, and cricket – if they win – and chasing women in that order. Years ago all pubs closed at 6 p.m. in the evening, and the number of drunks rolling around the streets was quite something.

The Aussie is shrewd, he's wary, unsophisticated, and has a deep highly suspicious inbred dislike for the smooth talking 'Limey' or 'Pommie', the Englishman.

He dislikes fancy talk, doesn't go a bomb on anything soph-isticated. He's the sort of chap who calls a spade a shovel. He's plain talking, and likes his 'Sheilas' to be the same. Enjoys sport the outdoor life, sunshine, surf-sea-sand, prefers the open spaces to any city. In many ways like his American counterpart, but doesn't have the natural charm of the Yank, the obvious liking the Yank shows about his doll.

Your Aussie likes his girl to be a 'good sport', that's very high praise indeed from him.

With an appetite that befits an athletic type of man, he's an impatient pursuer, who enjoys the game, the chasing, but hasn't the temperament to go for a long pursuit he likes to conquer, and not waste too much time getting there.

He's extremely, very sensitive about his accent, one thing you must not do, is to poke fun at it. It's no stranger than a Geordie's, a Welsh, a Devon or Scots accent, but as these others are all housed together in one island, they accept the wise-cracks, the fun poked at them from time to time. As Australia is geographically so far away, a certain sensitivity creeps in, if a remark is biased against the standard Australian accent.

An Aussie can be very off-hand with his 'Sheila', it's part of the accepted male, chauvinistic picture. He must at all times appear, butch, the swaggering male, drinking beer with his mates, with the little woman in attendance. Macho, that's the operative word, he must at all times be the dominant partner, that's part of his image, if it isn't he'll soon make it so.

The best way to handle your Aussie boy-friend, is to be feminine, at all times, this he likes. Wear perfume, and go in for sport, any kind.

You'll be expected to 'spoil' this very chauvinistic male – (if you come from Scotland or Wales, you'll have had some training) – attending to his needs, is expected. He'll never offer to do the dishes or any household chores, that's strictly female country, and leaves it at that.

His sense of humour, generally speaking, is pretty coarse, loud, bawdy, near the knuckle, a throwback to the type of humour around during Victorian Music-hall days. There are, thank heaven exceptions, but not many. Here's an example of a typical joke enjoyed by Aussie men.

Late Friday afternoon, a college senior in Sydney, dropped by the campus drug-store, and purchased three dozen prophylactics.

On Monday morning, he returned to the drug store, and in a loud voice complained: 'Last Friday, I came here and bought 3 dozen prophylactics and you only gave me 24.

'I'm very sorry sir,' said the pharmacist, handing him the extra dozen, 'I do hope we didn't spoil your weekend.'

Exercise, indoor or outdoor, is a big part of an Aussie's lifestyle. Jumping over chairs and landing on a double bed, when the chase is successfully concluded, that is considered the 'norm' Australian weekend, for red-blooded males, and there isn't a Sheila living who can hope to change this pattern for living.

My advice to any young maiden is this. Aussies believe in a very, very, short courtship, like one night, or just maybe, two.

So! unless it is a love greater than both of you I suggest one of you emigrate – quickly!

✳ ✳ ✳ ✳ ✳ ✳ ✳ ✳ ✳ ✳

I am told that the Australian male's very favourite story is the following, this will surely be a guide-line to any young lady, contemplating a permanent partnership with a fellow from 'down under!

The danger of using an elephant's trunk as the replacement, in the ultimate organ transplant is that when you're sitting in a restaurant, you never know when it will reach out, and grab a bun from the table.

◉ ◉ ◉ ◉ ◉ ◉ ◉ ◉ ◉ ◉ ◉

Jewish

Jewish men love the ladies and make no bones about it (most of them, that is). Next to business, my fair lady gets most of his attention and time. He thoroughly enjoys female company, seeks it whenever possible.

Unlike the British – English – Irish – Welsh – Scottish – American and Australian, whose priority is cricket – football – rugby – soccer – baseball and surfing, the jewish chap doesn't go over the top about sport. His hobby is the ladies the younger, the prettier, the better. 'So tell me where's the persentage in chasing a ball around a field? Where's the return. Me? I'd rather chase a pretty woman, one who does not run too fast.'

They differ only superficially from country to country, fundamentally very little. The American Jew might be more gregarious, more out-going, his British counterpart, reserved and conservative, but their tastes are comparable. Jewish women are a dominant part of the home, Mama has a great influence with her sons, and right through their lives the female plays an integral part in the life of the man.

They like to indulge the female, most of them are generous when pursuing their target, they splash out, the best is only good enough. They believe man was made for woman, and vice versa, still the best arrangement in town, and like good food, to be enjoyed as often as possible, a healthy appetite for sex is just part of the good life.

Not necessarily the most skilled of lovers, but far more experienced than your average male, he'll not count the cost, but, as a good business man wants a healthy return for his investment. You'll not fool this man with a 'headache' or a 'migraine'. He'll put you in touch with the best doctor in town, at a reduced rate of course, who'll cure you pronto, and you'll have no excuse.

He's a business man always. First he'll invest. Flowers, a show, plenty of good nosh, 'treat a woman like a princess' pamper her, be her knight in shining armour. If she's fat, tell her, threaten her, that if she loses just one ounce he'll give up cigars, (she'll love that). If she's on the lean side, tell her she

71

and Princess Diana are identical. Myron or Abe will flatter, praise, use lavish compliments, every trick in the book, so keep a cool mind with this charmer, he's like all men, anxious to please, before he presents the bill.

He will find a girl's preferences, your favourite wine, he'll get you lingerie and blouses wholesale – there is nothing he won't do to make you happy. And after a marvellous meal at Chow Ling's he'll wrestle like an octopus in the taxi, his hands all over your lily-white body, on your way home.

You need skill, a thick skin in handling this man. After all, if he doesn't care for cricket, doesn't go a bomb on soccer or rugby, he's got to be good at something and he is – females. He studies the opposite sex, and becomes an expert – with Myron wear high button blouses or better still, a one-piece jump suit that takes at least ten minutes to get on, and much longer to get out of. Hunting a female is one of life's great sports. The Jewish chap is in it to win, but, he doesn't always get the prize.

Irving lived in New York. He was part of the family business, clothing manufacturers on 7th Avenue, New York, or the 'Garment District' as it is more commonly known. Aggressive, successful, he met many models and other attractive women through his work. Irving had a penchant for the long legged model species, dated every night. His motto 'Work hard, play hard'. He did.

A short, stocky man, pleasant looking, his date usually towered over him. Despite this he had a great sense of humour, loads of patience and very necessary, plenty of money. He went all out in wooing his dolls and had a track record which Warren Beatty could envy, that is, until he met and fell head over heels for Ginny.

A genuine red-head, with long legs, a true American beauty, Ginny bowled him over, she was Irving's dream girl come to life. He wooed her in style. First nights, horse-racing, dining at New York's finest restaurants. Bowling or gambling. He sent flowers and funny gifts. A stuffed parrot that talked when wound up, its eyes whirling, he planned all kinds of surprises.

Ginny enjoyed herself. Irving was a lot of fun, gave her a good time, without coming on heavy. She wasn't physically attracted to him, knew it wouldn't last, his eyes devoured her every time they dated, but, it was good while it lasted.

Inevitably he started making overtures. How about getting away from the fumes of Manhatten, for some sea breezes in

73

Atlantic City? Irving coaxed, teased, pleaded, always in joke, and when she was most vulnerable. Ginny, who modelled, was feeling very tired, the sea sounded great, she said she'd think about it.

Unexpectedly, a week later, over dinner, she said she'd agree on conditions. Separate rooms, and four bottles of Moet Chandon champagne. Irving was over the moon, four, she could have four dozen if she wanted. No! the other condition was that they drink the four bottles before any hanky-panky. Irving's heart sank, all four? Yep, or no deal. But, he had no choice, he'd drink soya sauce if it meant claiming Ginny his dream girl.

They left late Friday afternoon. After checking in, they dined, saw a floor show, gambled at a Casino, then went back to Irving's room. Three bottles of champagne were lined up like soldiers, the fourth in a silver bucket, glasses on the side. Irving had refrained from drinking all night, now he was in a hurry to finish all four bottles. Glass for glass each started drinking, making jokes, laughing, the second bottle was opened. Eagerly, Irving downed his first glass, the second, the third, then slowed down, he was feeling mellow, happy. Ginny slapped him as he reached for her 'Hands off'.

Back to the serious business of drinking. Ginny opened the third bottle with a loud pop, poured out two more full glasses. Irving was getting sleepy, boy this wasn't as easy as he thought it would be. He knocked another glass down, and slid to the carpet. Ginny smiled at him, 'Come on Irving we've got quite a few glasses to go yet.' Lover boy shook his head and, with a sigh, closed his eyes and fell asleep. Ginny reached for a blanket, put it over him, picked up the unopened bottle of champagne, quietly letting herself out. She went to her room, collected her overnight bag, her coat and handbag and phoned for the reception to call her a cab.

At reception she left a typed envelope for Irving, her message was:

> Here's to you, whoever you may be,
> You're just a man of the moment, and nothing
>   more to me,
> If I should drink your liquor and get a wee bit
>   tight,
> Here's hoping you play the gentleman, and
>   take me home tonight
> But if your liquor should conquer,

And I fail the final test,
Here's one more drink to your technique,
You're a BETTER man than the rest

Ginny.

She said later, 'There was no way he was going to make it.
Irving never was a drinker, he couldn't handle it. Besides, he
believed in keeping himself clear-headed, ready for the
desert – me! Just this time, I trumped his ace. It's an old game
men use all the time, getting the girl tanked up, then seducing
her. I merely reversed the roles and let him keep his virginity.
It's what's called – strategy.'

Chauvinistic men have no qualms at all about using women.
Your lover-boy will promise you the earth, make all sorts of
plans for the future, he has not the slightest intention of keeping. All this is part of wooing a maiden, the minute a woman
surrenders herself to him, he's the one who calls the shots. As
soon as he gets bored, he looks for another playmate. So the
answer lies with us females. Keep him hunting. Promise –
promise – promise, but never ever deliver. If the situation gets
desperate – emigrate, if it's only for six months. Unless he
really agrees to tie the knot and, if that is what you want, great.

Once legally tied, your Jewish fellow is a good provider.
He'll play around given the chance, if there isn't a chance, he'll
make one. But you can rely on him to pay the rent, bring home
the lox 'n bagels, smoked salmon, a bottle of wine, as well as
a few dresses – wholesale.

Myron and Becky Cohen lived in New York, a pent-
house apartment on 5th Avenue, on the 65th floor. The
morning of their golden anniversary, Becky was up
early, went into the kitchen, and returned with a silver
tray, coffee, a single red rose in a silver holder, she tip-
toes to Myron's bedside.
'Vakey-vakey-My-ron, time to get up . . .'
'Go avay Becky, I need my schleep . . .'
'Vake up, My-ron, today is a very special day . . . and
I've got a leetle present for yo-hoooo.'
Myron sits up grumbling and sips his coffee.
'Now I vant you should put on your schlippers, mit the
tassels, your velvet collared dressing-gown and com met
me to the vindow . . .'
Still grumbling Myron does as he is told.
'Now! Vat do you see outside the vindow my Myron?'

75

'Becky at 9 o'clock in the morning I'm seeing vat I see every morning, the sky, the boirds, clouds, vat should I be seeing?'
'Myron, vat is lookin' straight at your nose from across the street?'
'Becky, lookin' at me from across the street is an apartment building . . . now can I go back to bed . . . ?'
'My-ron . . . that apartment building, lock, schtock 'n barrel and wreppted up in ribbons, is mine vedding anniversary present to you-hooooo.' Myron looks at her disbelievingly!
'That apartment building costs over a million bucks, Becky, vere vould you get that kind of money?'
Becky sighs a happy smile, her eyes glazed by memories . . .
'Do you remember our honeymoon in Atlantic City, nearly 40 years ago, Myron? Vell, ve had a little agreement, every time ve had a ROMP I put some monee in the kitty . . . I saved my monee, Myron, now that apartment building is for you . . . hoooo.'
Myron puts his head in his hands and moans and groans . . .
'Oi . . . Oi . . . Oi . . . Oi . . . Oi . . .'
Becky pats his shoulder,
'It's paid for, My-ron, lock schtock 'n barrel, wreppted up in ribbons . . .'
Myron groans and moans . . .
'Oi . . . Oi-Oi, Becky . . . Becky . . . if I'd only known, I'd have given you ALL mine business!'

A woman is much like a business, pick a good one, and you get lucky, pick a woman who doesn't play ball and you pay the price. But then life's a gamble anytime.
So? What else is new?

◎ ◎ ◎ ◎ ◎ ◎ ◎ ◎ ◎ ◎ ◎

Latins

Rudolph Valentino has a lot to answer for. Ever since he rode across the silver screen, on his white charger, women have dreamt of a dark, handsome sheik, who will one day come into their life, and sweep them off their feet.

Valentino was around in the 20's, but every time they show old movies, a new generation of females start dreaming about a man, with dark smouldering eyes, a turban around his head, riding breeches, boots, his shirt open at the chest. He moves swiftly, picks up the dreaming maiden, suddenly jumping on the white horse, parked at the curb-side, they ride off together, down the M4: M5: M6: into the sunset, and away into the desert and paradise.

What a lot of old cobbles.

The truth about Latins is very different indeed. Most of them are waiters, to be found in Soho restaurants. They are medium height, with bad teeth, which is one of the reasons they come to Britain, to get them fixed on the N.H.S. at our expense!

Greeks: Italians: Spanish: they have, mostly, black hair, brushed sleekly back, a big welcoming smile, which many of them hope will devastate some rich, American lady touring the U.K. and get them invited away for a cruise, or at least a weekend in Llandudno.

Away from work, they are trendy dressers, smell of a mixture of aftershave, garlic, 'n peppermints. They make much of kissing a fair lady's hand, there are two reasons for this. (1) It's considered very romantic, the local Brit wouldn't be caught dead doing it. (2) It gives him a chance to examine the ring, and check whether the diamonds are real or phoney.

The accent is pure schmaltz. Poured on like syrup, it sends some females into ecstasies. It sends others around the bend. Nevertheless, the Latins have such a fascination for many Brit maidens, that when they go into their routine, 'you ar-re so beauti-ful, your eyes ar-re like joowels . . .', another fair maiden is conquered.

The reason why these Latin lovers come to Britain generally speaking is: (1) To learn the language. (2) To meet a rich

woman. (3) To seduce as many of our virgins as his permit permits.

If a young lady will remember the above reasons, she can avoid a lot of heartache. When a Latin woos a young, fair Brit, he puts his conscience on 'Hold'. Courting a female takes time, effort and skill, so there's no point in confusing the issues, by being truthful. The latin lover, when passion overcomes his senses, pours out a stream of Spanish or Greek, whispering into the shell-like ear of his lady, usually its just a family recipe for potatoe salad, but she thinks, they are words of love.

Now for the real unvarnished truth!

Latin Lovers are an unlisted export from several countries. Each country has a different reason. The Spanish, although they would indignantly deny it, send their Casanova's to Britain for one express purpose.

Spain have never, ever, forgiven England, for Sir Francis' Drake's humiliation of the Spanish Armada. They have plotted for years to get even, and put the perfect answer into operation, many years ago.

For decades the 'Spaniard's Revenge' as it is called has been working. Handsome young Spaniards are sent to England, they come over here in droves during our summer, for one specific purpose. To woo our Catholic virgins, and, any pretty Protestant ones, seduce them, make sure they are pregnant, then return to Spain, to continue the good work with our girls who go over there for a holiday.

Many a sweet English 'miss' has returned from sunny Spain, with more than she bargained for.

This dastardly plan is quite simple. To flood, out-number the Brits, with Spanish bastards, thus conquering the hated enemy – England – legitimately. The Government is helpless to intervene, as passion and romance are beyond their jurisdiction, yet they must foot the bill for the upbringing of these Spanish 'moments of passion'!

The Greek Government also have a plan, also against England, but their objective is slightly different.

For years now, a blonde ex-actress, holding the office of Cultural Minister in the Greek government, has been actively agitating, pressing, and doing everything she can, to get Britain to return the Elgin Marbles to Greece.

To the uninitiated, they are not those round little glass balls that the kids in school play with. They are classical figures, carved in marble, that Lord Elgin brought back to England a long time ago. Now this Greek lady wants them back.

So far nothing doing, once we start down that road, who knows where it will end.

Wales could rightly claim the throne of England, on the grounds that as there was no heir to Elizabeth 1st, a Celt through her father and grandfather – Henry VIth, and therefore only a true Celt should sit on the throne. Scotland could resume battle, and claim stolen land, titles, jewels, the list is endless. Ireland has such a long list, there isn't time to mention her authentic claims.

My Uncle Willie says, it's a very dangerous precedent, there's no knowing where it'll stop. 'I mean, if the French ever find out about that nude figure I took from a place I visited in Bordeaux, when I was over there in World War I, there'll be a real war in the valleys. She, the missus, thinks it's a work of art I bought from Rouen Cathedral.'

Long ago, Italy started out with a specific plan, but that was about 19 governments ago, and the original reasons for sending so many of their men to England has been lost in the shuffle of so many changes in high office.

They too decided that as we – the Brits – were the enemy in the last war, they would punish us.

They have been partly successful too. All over Wales, England, Scotland, you'll find Ice-cream parlours with names like: Canoletti: Garabaldi: there are so many Antonio's – Tony's, and that too was part of a master-plan. To flood Britain with ice-cream. And they almost got away with it, their sons marrying local girls, strengthening the Italian connection, producing more sons for the mother country.

The English aren't as dim-witted as some of their enemies make out they are. They can spot a winner, and take appropriate action.

One Italian did so well here with his ice-cream, he expanded, went into all kinds of business. The English moved fast. They knighed him, he became a 'Sir' then elevated to 'Lord', and is now a peer of the realm, an English subject. As an old Yorkshire fellow said, 'Ay . . . we might look stupid, but that don't mean we're daft!'

Try this test with your Greek suitor.

Just as he thinks he's winning, and you're beginning to tingle under the arm-pits, say very casually, 'So tell me, Pericles, what's your stand on the Elgin Marbles then?' If he starts discussing the merits of the 'marbles' drink your 'Ooozee' and run, you can be sure he's a phoney.

Spaniards are proud passionate people, with very long

80

memories. All you need do with Don Carlos, and it'll take courage, is lift your glass, look him straight in the eye, but smile, and say, 'A toast to Sir Francis Drake.' If, and I say, if, he smiles and toasts our great sailor, he could be genuine, and not after your weekly Social Security cheque. However, the chances are pretty remote! He will, I suspect, be very angry, he might whip out his sword, most Spaniards carry one, and very likely challenge you to a duel.

Just dive under the table, this is no time to be brave and wait until he cools down, then exit, and I do mean fast.

With Italians, it's straightforward lust, but all these latin lovers are tigers when aroused, so here is a tried and tested method to cool the ardour of the most passionate of Latin lotharios.

Stick a segment of garlic into your hand-bag. When you feel danger is close at hand, make the usual excuse and go to the 'ladies'. Chew on your segment, by the time you get into the taxi, your breath will not only keep him right over in his corner seat, don't be surprised if when the cab stops at a red light, he jumps out, without even saying 'goodbye'.

It's like General Montgomery said:

'War is all a matter of strategy.'

⊙ ⊙ ⊙ ⊙ ⊙ ⊙ ⊙ ⊙ ⊙ ⊙

Professional Men

Members of Parliament

They are addressed in the House of Commons as 'The Right Honourable Gentleman' – which brought this comment from an old wag, 'Start the day with a laugh, that's what I say.'

Some of the finest con-men in the nation park their posteriors on the blue-plush seats of the House. Our M.P. sits wrapped happily in a fog of smug satisfaction, pondering on the good fortune that brought it all about and praying fervently that those who sent him there will not discover the truth about him, until he is safely re-elected for another term.

Every shape, every size, from differing backgrounds, they, the élite, are the Right Hon. Members of Parliament put there to represent you and me, voted democratically to look after our interests.

No! This is not a fairy story.

Their biggest asset is the ability to convince the likes of you and me in believing them, when they say their only and most sincere desire is to better our lives and to solve our little problems.

So, how come our local M.P. swore on a stack of political speeches he personally would see to it that Harry Higgens' rabbit hutch down in the allotment would be repaired before winter set in and Harry is still waiting after 4 years. Not only that, but he hasn't even seen the M.P. since.

NEVER BELIEVE ANYTHING SAID BY AN M.P.

If you are being wooed, chased, romanced by an M.P., keep that advice firmly in mind. As you dine on oysters and he presses you to have another port 'n lemon and whispers sweet nothings in your ear, remember Harry Higgens and his rabbit hutch.

They mean well, but when an M.P. is born, part of his body is missing, he doesn't have a conscience. He thoroughly enjoys female company, but has reservations about the type of woman he'll go out with. Your M.P. hero likes his women dumb, not too much brain-matter. He believes one brain in the family is enough, he can't stand the brainy type – females who think. If he had his way, they wouldn't be allowed to vote. He's not chauvinistic and would be genuinely astonished if you accused him of such beliefs. He honestly believes a woman should be decorative, charming, good cook, available for a romantic skirmish, when the mood takes him.

Many, many M.P.'s hold the same beliefs. They simply cannot come to terms with a woman in politics. One M.P. of years standing, still is unable to accept that we have a woman Prime Minister. He's turned up drunk every day he's attended holding the hope that one day the Sergeant-at-Arms will tap him on the shoulder and say, 'It's alright, sir, we've got a man now.'

The real danger in dating an M.P. is his skill. After all, if he can fool thousands into voting for him in believing his far-fetched promises, what chance have you, when he turns the force of his lethal charm on just one slip of a girl?

So, how to handle this slippery, tricky customer? You find his weakness and play on it, you've got no real problem. Like the Yanks say, 'It's just like taking candy from a baby.'

If you find yourself in a difficult situation, when passion rears its head and his only conversation is in braille, try this, but first a question.

What is my M.P.'s favourite topic?

Politics?   NO!

Ambition?   NO!

HIMSELF?   YES!

The minute you feel you can't control the situation, switch the subject to him. Get him talking about himself and your troubles are over, you can relax. He'll be perfectly happy, provided you do not interrupt him.

M.P.'s generally are a much easier type to handle than any other male, if you bear in mind that he got where he is using bluff and promises, then turn the tables, by using his own methods. Promise, promise, giving no guarantee of a delivery date.

One successful model, a pretty blonde, kept a Tory M.P. at bay for over six months. She explained she was being cured by her Psychiatrist with regular treatments, sessions of healing, regarding a rare mental disorder and under no circumstances was she to have any physical contact with the opposite sex until he pronounced her well and until such time they would have to be 'just friends'. It worked, beautifully.

Actresses make the best wives for M.P.'s for the simple reason, becoming an M.P.'s wife calls for acting skills, in other words you'll have to play many roles successfully. Mistress,

86

Wife, Secretary, Chauffeur, Mother. 'Drop everything let's go' is a well known order, and you do.

He's never yours, not the M.P., he belongs to many people, he's public property in a sense, a servant of the people who put him where he is, a seat of power in Westminster.

Mind you, some M.P.'s go too far in pleasing their constituents. Here's a true story which illustrates my point.

This happened during the hectic canvassing, before the last election. Candidates called non-stop at the house of one well-endowed lady, a lady with no taste for politics, a husband in Saudi Arabia and nothing but time on her hands.

With so many people trying to convince her that the only party to vote for was theirs, she decided to put them through her own kind of test.

The Tory man called, asked in and after some chat about politics, she invited him to see her new curtains and carpet in the bedroom. Later, straightening his tie, waving goodbye, he bid her farewell, wishing all his would-be constituents could be attractive.

The SDP candidate called, was also given some tea, asked what was he going to do for her? Invited to see her new curtains/carpets but as she put her hand on his thigh, caressingly, he fled, spilling the tea all over the table.

The Labour candidate was last and responded with alacrity at her invitation, where for one hour in her bedroom, he let her know why Labour was best.

A roving reporter chanced to interview this lady at a shopping centre a few days later regarding her political opinion, whom did she favour? 'Labour, of course.' Asked to give her reasons, replied: 'They are triers, aren't they?' Asked to clarify this remark, she said, 'Well look at it this way, the Tories are willing, but you don't hear from them again, the SDP, they're all talk, but no action, but the Labour chap gives his all and he calls again and again. Any chap who persists and calls, who cares . . . well he's got to win.' The roving reporter still can't figure out what she was trying to say.

The following was my Dad's favourite story.

A hard-working mother, left a widow, struggled to educate her four children – four sons.

Working all hours, all kinds of jobs, she managed to give them a good schooling, all but her youngest son who had contacted a virus which left him with permanent brain damage.

Many years later, her sons now grown-up men, she was declared 'Mother of the Year', the Mayor himself presenting her with flowers and a cheque.

'Tell me, Mrs Fairbrother, how are your sons, where are they?' Proudly the mother told him, 'My 1st son is a judge. My 2nd a Banker, my 3rd a Lecturer at Oxford University.' The Mayor shook her hand, 'What a credit to you, and to the sacrifice, the hard work you did, but tell me, how is your youngest son, is he any better now?' The mother smiled broadly, 'Heavens to be, Mr Mayor, you are behind with the news. My Bob is an M.P. in London, doing a very successful job at it too!'

Marrying an M.P. is no joke, fun maybe, but no joke. You need guts, courage, real courage, the stamina of a bull, strength of an Ox, the dedication of a mother determined to marry off her 'old maid' daughter. These are just some of the qualities, you have to have, then you've got a fighting chance, to take on and handle this most slippery of men. It's a life sentence, but, some women, a rare few, are still around to prove there is a life, after the House of Commons has faded into the mists of memory.

★ ★ ★ ★ ★ ★ ★ ★ ★ ★

SHORT TRIBUTE

A man came to the Golden Gate
His head was bent and low
He meekly asked the Man in White
Which way he was to go?

'What have you done?' St Peter asked
'What was your earthly task?'
'I was Speaker at the House of Commons sir
from daybreak until dusk!'

St Peter opened wide the Gate
He gently pressed the bell
'Come in and choose your harp, good man
You've had *your* share of Hell!'

◉ ◉ ◉ ◉ ◉ ◉ ◉ ◉ ◉ ◉

Farmers

'HANDLE WITH CARE' that label should be pinned upon every farmer, when he goes a-wooing, and with good reason too.

Just as the discipline from army life sticks to a soldier long after he's left the service, an accountant mentally tabulates the cost of everything on holiday, or at a wedding. So it is with a farmer, the years of working close to nature leaves its distinctive mark upon him and there-in lies the danger, for the opposite sex.

Figure it out for yourself.

All day every day, week in, week out he is surrounded by animals. Pigs, sheep, cows and bulls, horses, dogs and cats, goats and chickens, ducks, all of them having it off – all responding to the 'call of nature'.

It's enough to drive a red-blooded male bonkers, it did just that to one farmer. We had farms all round us where I lived as a girl, and one farmer was a man named Trevor Turnbull.

Trevor was built like a bull. Strong, red-faced, he could pull up a tree. His favourite pastime was wenching, and he was apparently a terror. Then he went and fell head over heels in love with Cora Armstrong, the daughter of a new tenant farmer who lived a mile or some from Trevor's farm.

Cora kept Trevor dangling alright; she knew all about his past, and wasn't about to become one of his victims. Then it happened, one hot summer's day – what triggered it off, no one knew; whether it was watching the bull chasing the cows or what?

Trevor jumped on his tractor, tore right through the hedge, clean across the lawn, across two fields, sheep and cows running left and right to get out of the way, and landed on the front lawn of the Armstrong farm. Shouting, he stormed into the house, but Cora saw him coming and ran into the haystack, Trevor caught a glimpse of her, ran after her quickly, bolting the barn door. Nine months later, after a shotgun wedding, Cora gave birth to a lovely bouncing baby boy.

That happened many years ago, and although it's not true to say that every farmer gets turned on every time a tomcat chases a pussycat, it is true that a farmer is far more aware of

the sexual needs of human nature than most men. They believe the animals have the right answer in 'Doing what comes naturally'.

A nice girl can't afford to take chances if she is going steady with a farmer. He gets unexpected urges, so its best to keep in well-lit places and make sure there are people about.

I was talking with a young married woman, Mary, now married to a vet, she told me about the time she was engaged to a farmer – Timothy. Never an easy man, hot tempered, but kind enough, liked getting his own way and didn't like being crossed. Well, they were attending his aunt's funeral, and he got that look in his eye. He demanded they go upstairs while the relatives were having the funeral tea downstairs. Mary couldn't believe her ears, but he was serious alright, and that finished that romance.

If you're dating a farmer, you've got to ask yourself, 'Is this what you really want?' It's not every girl's idea of paradise, but it does have a lot of perks. For instance, you are guaranteed a turkey every Christmas, all the eggs you can eat, milk, fresh vegetables and fresh air. You've never seen a skinny farmer or a farmer's wife who doesn't look well fed, they don't exist. Come the tsetse fly, floods, the black plague, your farmer always eats well.

Meeting a farmer 'on the town' is meeting a man on his best behaviour, so don't get taken in by his 'gentle touch' approach. He uses this on sick animals, a lamb, a lame horse, a bird, soothing, gently calming down the little patient, lulling the senses with kind, comforting words, like a good doctor.

With you, however, the end result means you caring for him, so watch his moves. I asked a mature farmer his opinion of the female. 'A woman is no different from a thoroughbred, you have to handle them both carefully, mustn't frighten or stampede the filly, can't be rushed. They've got to be coaxed, gentled along, but once you've gained mastery over them, there is no problem . . . mind you, can't let go of the reins, you've got to show them who's boss . . .'

The chauvinistic farmer's point of view.

A farmer's wife gave me her opinion. 'Think of him as a stallion. Hot-blooded, determined to get his own way, that was my first impression of Willet, my husband. A farmer is a special breed of man, you've got to know how to handle him. Willet didn't believe in wasting time. 'Fancying up a woman' that's what he called it. He made it plain, he wanted to, let's say 'sample the goods' before putting down a deposit.

91

She laughed, 'He tried every kind of trick, but I'm country born 'n bred myself, so I was prepared, but he was a real handful. Willet enjoyed the company of women, but had no intention of giving up his bachelor status, playing the field was more fun. We went on picnics, and I remember one warm afternoon, things were getting out of hand, I was very much in love and thought, "what can I do?" Then I shrieked and sat up . . . a snake . . . a snake. I pointed to the undergrowth . . . "It's in there."

Willet looked astounded. 'But there's no snakes, my lovely one, here . . .' By that time I was on my feet walking away laughing with my back to Willet. 'Come back, sweetheart . . .' I kept on walking, saved once again.

After several months, Willet was frustrated, cross, but unwilling to commit himself, and I wasn't prepared to settle for less than marriage. I then played my trump card.

One afternoon looking my best in a blue flowered dress, perfumed, my hair all curly and my face white with powder, I needed to look paler than pale, I did. Choosing the time and place, I told Willet I had galloping consumption, and the doctor said it was serious.

The doctor recommended marriage, and as Stan Brewer – the solicitor – was very keen, I was considering whether to accept his proposal (pure fiction) and thought it only fair under the circumstances to tell Willet before going ahead.

It worked too. Willet knew Stan Brewer was keen, he also knew the game was up. He proposed there and then, we were married in six months, and been together over thirty years, and I still don't know what galloping consumption is?

Be prepared, go into battle, and be prepared for a tricky courtship, and if he's what you want – practise going to bed early and getting up early, that's what a farmer's life is all about – well almost.

A farmer went to market and bought a rooster to keep his hens happy, on arriving home he set the rooster loose, to see how happy he could make them. The rooster immediately went on the rampage around the farmyard. Arising early the next morning, the farmer found that in fact none of his livestock had been spared – pigs, cows, sheep, all had been subjected to the rooster's appetite – but the rooster himself could not be found. The farmer searched all morning, and at last found the rooster stretched out, gasping and groaning, in the middle of his

largest field, with half a dozen vultures circling over-
head. The farmer cried, 'See what you get, at it all night,
and now you've done yourself in.' Whereupon the rooster pointed skywards and said:
    'Sshhhhhhhh . . .!'

If you do find yourself married to a farmer, and lots of sane
pleasant women have gone this route, the best way to handle
him is, think of him as part of the stock. For example, you
could be baking an apple pie, preparing jellies, and he'll walk
in, hay sticking out of his hair, smelling of pig manure, breathing heavily, saying he's hungry, sweat glistening on his brow,
his face browned by the sun. Take a good look at the
expression in his eyes, when a farmer says he's hungry – it
doesn't necessarily mean he wants roast beef and gravy More
than likely he's watched the rooster or the bull getting some
action, dropped everything, some farmers have been known
to rush into the house in the middle of milking – they've got
so excited.

So take this friendly warning. If you're thinking of tying up
with a farmer for keeps, make very sure you love animals. Go
to 'keep fit classes' months before the wedding, and keep a
large jar of salt petre on the mantlepiece. (They use this to
dampen down the sex urge in prisons.) Only don't use it too
often, you just might get used to being chased 'up them stairs'
at unexpected moments, and you could even get to like it!

    ⊙ ⊙ ⊙ ⊙ ⊙ ⊙ ⊙ ⊙ ⊙ ⊙

Chauvinistic

Chauvinistic men are men with an inferiority complex. Find a man who talks down to women, dismisses their opinions as worthless, treats them as 'females', and you find a man who is inadequate, a bully, and quite likely, a braggart. His motto reads:

'A WOMAN IS JUST A WOMAN
BUT A GLASS OF BEER IS SHEER PLEASURE'

No man can fake being a gentleman, it's a quality that defies sham. Many put on an act but – it's just that, the mask slips, the real ego is easily detected.

The chauvinistic male is found in large numbers in Wales, Ireland, Scotland, and in the North of England. Women who live with these men are always second-class females, he the male makes sure of that. But, the fault often lies in the woman herself, especially 'dear old Mam'. Mother has always put Dad and his wishes, his welfare, first. When Sonny-boy starts growing up, he, being male, gets the same special treatment, and what a prize pig he turns out to be, a real gift for some unsuspecting young bride.

'My mother always cooked rice this way . . .' 'Why my Mam never thought twice about . . . she just did it . . .'

To throw off the shackles, that have bound women to this pathetic myth – that, MAN is MASTER – takes time and patience. With the world now shrinking in size, education right outside the front door, in night-classes, lectures, scholarships, it's easier for the female to reach out, and equip herself, at least professionally, with the know-how that can get them into positions of authority.

One of the reasons it's such a joy to live in the USA, and why Europeans and British men, are so scathing in their denunciation of the American male, is American men DARE to treat women with respect; they openly acknowledge their intelligence. This to many Brits is not only outrageous, but an unforgiveable act of treachery. Putting females on a pedestal, treating them as a pretty little thing, to be given presents, petted or even loved, is acceptable; but to actually give acknowledgement that they have *brains* is an act of heresy, not only to be condemned, but the traitor who behaves thus, to be treated with the utmost contempt, by his fellow men.

This is one reason, a strong one too, why you'll seldom, ever, hear a Britisher – male – say anything favourable about his American cousin – (except his own kind, and they exist in the USA too).

I know a man – don't we all? – who publicly treats all females, his wife included, with barely concealed contempt, in front of his male associates. But, like the coward this type is, once behind four walls, in his own house, he crawls, asking forgiveness, happy to do any menial job, to make amends for his public behaviour.

An attractive Welsh lady was telling me about her husband, another 'Mam's boy'. This chauvinistic male goes drinking with the boys, most nights, but when she says, she'll pop over to visit a friend he wants to know, Why? What for? Woman, in 1986, actually have to explain, ask permission from their chauvinistic keepers, before they can do the most ordinary thing, like visiting with a friend.

A manly man, the kind of male who is considerate to the opposite sex, who holds all women in regard, wouldn't be associated with the chauvinistic pig specimen, he abhors such behaviour. It's not difficult to understand.

The chauvinists run in packs. Whether they are leather-clad, motor-cycle types, who meet in pubs. Or the more sober-clad Saville Row suited men, who meet in Clubs, under the skin, they are all blood brothers.

Individually they are cowards, it is only when they out-number their opposition that they find any courage – is that what they call it? – and how we all enjoy seeing this sort get their come-uppance.

A mild mannered lorry-driver had been provoked for the past few weeks every time he stopped at a road-side cafe for a meal, by three 'hell's Angels'.

This day was no exception, as soon as he was seated, eating his meal, they walked in. The first one went over to his table, picked up some of his chips, ate them, and walked away. The second did the same, picking a nice piece of bacon, dipping it in sauce and walked away, and the third, reached over, took his sausage, chewed it, and walked away.

96

Throughout all this the driver paid no attention, when he finished he paid for his meal, and left the cafe.

The leather-clad leader said to the cafe owner, 'He's not much of a man, he didn't put up any fight at all.' 'He's not much of a driver either,' said the owner, 'he's just flattened three motor-bikes.'

Any woman needs a good, strong, sense of humour to handle this breed, for truly they are to be pitied. Pathetic creatures, we really should feel sorry for them, as one would be to a crippled bird or dog. They know they are inadequate, fearful of anyone finding out the truth, so to compensate they hit back, physically or verbally and it's always at those who are in no position to hit back, or defend themselves.

A woman must use whatever weapon she can, and a clever woman can often take sweet revenge.

Back in my New York days, one of my friends was a stunning blonde, called Peg. She was one of the kindest, most generous people I've ever met. Peggy was from the deep South – she could charm a canary right out of its cage. Add good looks, a sense of fun, and you have one of the most popular gals in town. Her admirers came from every walk of life. The one thing that would arouse Peg to absolute fury was to see anyone ill-treated, or put-down.

A South-American diplomat visited new York, met Peg at a party. He was rich, very attractive, very charming. He treated all women as ladies, with old-fashioned courtesy and respect. He treated servants, waiters, porters, chauffeurs, with arrogance and disdain. Peg said, 'More than once I nearly hit him, but bided my time.'

After a week, of wining, dining – dancing, romancing, it was time for Peg's Latin-lover to return home. He asked Peg, the day before leaving, if she would be kind enough to pick up some extra special gifts, for his wife and daughter, and said casually to pick up a little 'something' for herself. He handed her his credit card, for one of New York's swankiest stores, and off Peggy went.

Friday noon, Peggy had bought the presents for her friend, and started on a shopping spree of her own. It took her right up to closing time, and even then she wasn't finished.

By 5.30 she had:15 pairs of shoes – Handcrafted.
6 sets of beautiful, cobwebby Negligee's: (Lace 'n silk.)
3 Overcoats: Tweed and fine Cashmere.
10 Blouses: Lingerie:

97

Complete set of luggage: 5 handbags; 3 Evening bags.
Pearls and two brooches: 6 bottles perfume: earrings.
5 Scarves in silk . . .

She had to stop as the store was being shut. It took two cabs
and three friends to help get the stuff to her apartment.

She had drinks with her Latin friend before he caught his
plane, handed him the gifts and his credit card. He thanked
her profusely for being such a wonderful friend and bade her
goodbye.

What he thought or said, when a bill for over 31,000 dollars
landed on his desk, has not been recorded, but as Peg said
with a wicked look in her eye, 'Maybe . . . just maybe, he'll
give bigger tips now to waiters and cabbies . . .'

The chauvinist male has to show off, he must buy a round,
an extra one, he must pick up the cheque at the restaurant,
he's just got to play the 'Big Man', and who eventually pays
for this? Right! The wife, and quite often, the children. They
go without, make do with last year's coat, no extras for a little
luxury, it doesn't matter what happens, HIS image is all that
counts.

One of the happiest stories I've heard is about a couple with
three children. He – BOSS-MAN – she, Slave, there to serve
her Lord 'n Master, that is how the dialogue went.

Everything in the house revolved around him, his moods,
his needs, his whims. He had to be considered first, everyone
else fitted in/around whatever he wished. His wife, put up
with much, like all caring mothers, the abuse, shortage of
necessities, his bullying, she bore it all, keeping her heartaches
to herself. The few pennies she managed to save, she occasionally played the football pools, just a one column attempt, and,
one day it happened. She won over £30,000 on the
pools. Her reaction was one of stunned astonishment, and
delight. Wisely, however, for the first time since being married, she opened a bank account in her own name.

She told her husband. At first he was overjoyed, and smiling
broadly, outlined plans to spend the money, his own needs
of course being first. When she said it was remaining in her
account he was furious. He threatened, bullied, coaxed, and
then – crawled. Anything, anything, she wanted, she only
had to ask. Hadn't he been a good, generous provider? He
brought home flowers, he gave the children chocolate – only
at Christmas had they had any before – he couldn't do enough
to please her, he planned for just the holiday the whole family

would have. And all the time, pleading for her to open a joint account.

Quietly, she told him, she would give it some thought, but made her own plans. She bought a small house. Furnished it with good second-hand furniture, bought curtains, until finally it was finished.

It was two months later, when the BOSS-man, ever attentive now, came home after a day at the office. The house sparkled, dinner was ready, she served it, he asked where was her's. Calmly she told him. The children were staying with friends, she was all packed, taking nothing with her, except her clothes, and, leaving him, setting up house with her children.

'You're on your own, the solicitor will be in touch. You can visit, and see the children whenever you wish. As you know, I'll not need any money.' She put the house keys on the table, and walked out before he could even speak.

Is it any wonder, why some women, going fifteen rounds with a chauvinistic male, says, 'Enough! No more, give me a key to my own little place, no matter how humble, my children, and peace, just peace.'

Amen! and a big thankful prayer for the real gents still around.

⊙ ⊙ ⊙ ⊙ ⊙ ⊙ ⊙ ⊙ ⊙ ⊙

Hotel

Hotel men whatever rank, owner, keeper, manager, are all born under the Sherlock Holmes sign, they are by nature a suspicious breed, suspecting the worse from their fellowman and check up on each other unhesitatingly.

Their slogan is:

'There's nowt so queer as folk, except thee and me, and, ah have me doobt about thee also.

Outwardly courteous, deferential, oily or haughty, depending upon the establishment and the number of slaves they command, your Top Man is always on guard, distrustful, watchful, prepared for the very worst. The human race is his personal cross, he never can relax, is on the lookout for clues, a tell-tale sign when guests check in.

I wouldn't go so far as to say that his staff give their guests a 3rd degree when they check in. They are instructed to wait until the guests have retired for the night, undressed, ready for bed, in curlers and shorts, then a knock at the door saying, 'It's your Ovaltine . . .' The little woman is so touched, 'What a kindly thought, Arthur,' then once in the room questions are asked to find out the nature of their visit, how long will they stay.

Its not the kind of welcome recommended by the Tourist Board, but it sure scares the pants off some and especially if the manager is dressed in what looks like the SAS uniform, pulls out a notebook, demanding to know date of birth and other details, while you are shivering in your jockey shorts and the wife in her see-through nightie.

Mind you, you'll often find, deep, deep down inside a kind, kind core.

One hotel manager, suffering from a bout of guilt (very rare) after holding a chap by his heels, dangling him out of a window with a 40ft drop, because he refused to tell whether he was C of E or Roman Catholic. The manager explained away the incident by saying the fellow was trying to pick some flowers, (even though the nearest daisy was 25ft away). The kind-hearted manager sent a basket of fruit to the hospital,

101

bananas, peaches, grapes, oranges, all kinds with get well wishes.

The little chap in hospital (managers never pick up big 'uns) sent word back. As soon as he was well enough, he and his 6ft brother would visit the hotel and personally stuff the manager with fruit, to show they too could be generous.

Not all managers are so obvious, or carry on like that. Most are controlled, impeccably behaved servants of the public! (That's a laugh right there.) They use more subtle ways to bring their guests to heel, if they don't measure up, to the hotel's standards. They gently, but firmly guide them in the right direction.

A lady checked into one establishment for a week. She stated her preference for scrambled eggs for breakfast. Now, the chef at this place, boiled all his eggs the night before, so he could have a bit of a lay-in in the morning, and did not want to be bothered with individual tastes. They went to work on the guest, trying to discourage her but she insisted, 'No! not boiled eggs – scrambled.' That was that! The manager, whose sister was married to the chef, talked the situation over with him. 'It's no good, Volari, she won't play ball.' The chef shrugged his shoulders, 'Ze usual treatment?' The manager nodded his assent.

Next morning, the lady was served a large helping of scrambled eggs. She tasted a mouthful, put her fork down, summoned the waiter. 'These eggs have a funny, horrid taste. Why?' 'Ah, Madam,' smirked the waiter, 'they are duck eggs.' 'Well take them back, I don't like duck eggs, get me chicken eggs. 'I'm so sorry, Madam, but our chef is temperamental, he won't scramble anything but duck eggs . . .' 'That is the most ridiculous thing I've ever heard . . .' The manager had to be sent for. He explained that their chef was very temperamental, impossible to replace as his cooking was beyond description, could they get Madam a lightly, lightly boiled egg. They did, she ate it, until she found by the end of the week they were as hard as bullets and she left.

Many types of men fancy this profession. An ex-Army chap used his money to buy a place in the country. Marvellous food, first-class accommodation, excellent service, but everyone was regimented. A bugle call, blown outside the bedrooms of not only the staff, but guests, rooms, awoke everyone with a shock. Anyone who went back to sleep and was late for breakfast or lunch were fined with 'extra service' tagged on the bill. All kinds of army drill was enforced, but when the Top Man

102

firmly insisted prunes and porridge for everyone, no excuse, the entire staff quit.

The only weapon a young girl, a woman, can use with success against this type of fellow, is a sense of humour, as they never possess one, you will find it invaluable, especially when they start to interrogate you. It's nothing personal mind you, it's part of their character.

Diane Gilbey was married to a chap in the trade. Enjoying a night off at their home, Diane told hubby she fancied some fish 'n chips and walked the ten-minute distance there. Finding a queue, she chatted with a neighbour's husband, enquired about the wife in hospital and he gallantly walked her home part of the way. When she got to the gate, her husband jumped out from behind the bushes, he'd been skulking there, waiting. Why was she so late? What kept her? How long had she been chatting to that man? Was there anything going on? Questions, suspicions.

Diane simply patted him on the hand, as she got the plates out. 'Before you go right over the top, Neville, let me explain. I met Neil Kinnock, who tried to persaude me to be the Labour candidate for our constituency, but I said no. Just as I started walking back, who do you think drove up in a Jag but Terry Wogan, he wanted me to co-present his show once a week. I tell you, Neville, everyone shows up at our local chippy . . .'

It's not generally known, but most hotel managers are rejects from M.5. But, take heart if you do intend to commit your life to one of this breed. Women marry policemen, some become head of Scotland Yard, they have to adapt and so will you – if you must! However, like I say, a sense of humour is ESSENTIAL. Buy one, rent one, but get one, you'll survive a hell of a lot longer if you do. After all, one of you should be in possession, it's for sure he won't be.

Talking to Mary, married for many, many years to her Manager husband, she remarked, that a sense of humour was a 'must', and told about her husband Ron, a good, fine man, but seldom saw the funny side of life. She gave me the following example.

Ron was due to speak at a Rotary meeting, and was very anxious to make a good impression. To his horror, a few minutes before the meeting was opened, his dentures broke.

'Don't worry about it,' said one of his acquaintances, 'I've a friend who will fix you up without bother.' Off he went and shortly returned with a choice of dentures. Ron was delighted to find a set that fitted him well, and saw him through the evening.

'That must be a wonderful dentist friend to have,' he said afterwards, 'to be able to fix me up like that.'

'He's no dentist,' came the reply, 'he's the undertaker.'

Ron still doesn't see the funny side.

◉ ◉ ◉ ◉ ◉ ◉ ◉ ◉ ◉ ◉ ◉

Psychiatrists

Psychiatrists are men with problems. They take up psychiatry, and listen to men and women who have problems. By listening to others, the psychiatrist's own worries and fears diminish, in comparison. That gives him a superior kind of knowledge which, in turn, qualifies him to give advice, charge a large fee to any patient who chooses to enjoy the privilege of lying down on a couch, in pleasant surroundings, and have someone like himself (who thinks he knows all the answers) listen to his rantings and ravings.

The above information was volunteered by a psychiatrist. It's big business in the USA. Catching on in the UK fast.

Today every large city has a white-coated gentleman, ready to listen to you or me, about any problem. If he is posh, he'll wear a suit, with a flower in his lapel. If you are a genuine nutcase or border-line, you can go on the National Health Service, and your doctor will then arrange a session for you, with his favourite 'shrink', as some of these gentlemen are often called, disrespectfully.

Lots of them are human beings themselves, and if you are currently dating a psychiatrist, there are some things you should know.

He is a very complex man, full of all kinds of phobias picked up from his patients, so be on guard, you too, don't get infected!

Be wary, he can be very tricky, charming, extremely understanding, he'll use his skills to lull you into a state of trust, just as you begin to feel secure Wham! you're at his mercy, and no escape.

Smooth and reassuring, it's part of his professional manner, a psychiatrist can make a girl feel, very, very, special, by just using his skill and knowledge. He'll find out what she thinks, what is in her heart's desire, it's just another ploy to get what he's after.

Mind you, many of them are completely mixed up themselves, and desperately in need of a good psychiatrist, just look for the signs.

One evening you're dining out with Dr Jekyll, next date

it's Mr Hyde. The change from the smooth, solicitous suitor, wrapped in you and your pleasure, starts with the amount of drink he consumes. He'll be nervous, anxious, and order wine, whisky, brandy, then a coffee to steady his nerves.

You will reverse places in your relationship, now it's your turn to comfort, console, hold his hand, be the understanding, sympathetic partner.

After several dates, and you are determined not to be emotionally involved, this is what you can expect.

He'll tell you he's had a rough, really tough day, order drinks, smile, soulful eyes gazing into yours. After the meal he'll say, 'I don't know what I'd do without you, my darling.' Later he'll come on strong, 'Why don't you stay overnight? I've plenty of room, the spare bedroom is all made up – please? I have these shocking migraines, they drive me mad, I can't sleep, pace up and down – if only you were there, just to talk to, I'd feel so much better, just being with you helps . . .!'

He's good alright, and so convincing. All that's needed is a violin in the background, scraping away, and you've got a scene right out of an old Bette Davis movie. Big soulful eyes, pleading, imploring.

What a performance! It's surprising how many women fall for this old routine, if you do, then you need a 'shrink' yourself.

Thankfully not every young lady is susceptible, some are very adept at handling the smooth, practised wolf.

A very attractive psychology student was dating a handsome young psychiatrist. He had quite a reputation with the fair sex, and an impressive score card.

He went into action, flowers, lunches, the theatre, a drive, all the usual things two people do together.

After a few weeks, and a romantic dinner, he felt it was time to get a closer relationship established.

He whispered in her ear, 'How about you and I going away together for a weekend in the country, a quiet and relaxing couple of days?'

'I'm afraid,' she answered, 'that my awareness of your proclivities in the esoteric aspect of sexual behaviour precludes such an erotic confrontation.'

'I don't get it,' he said.

'Precisely,' was her reply.

'He never dated her again.'

A psychiatrist is a man with a map about human behaviour,

107

he can read signs, he knows a great deal about human weakness, and he'll play upon them, especially if he's courting a girl. If you resist his advances, he can make gentle fun, by telling you to 'be adult' – don't fall for that. Translation – surrender, girl, surrender. Don't however be alarmed when the chips are down, he's just another male trying to figure out the age-old riddle, what makes females tick?

Another advantage. You can behave as irrationally as you wish, and he'll put it down to another quirk in human behaviour. If the going gets too rough, try this.

A well-known Hollywood actress had been through a very emotional time, what with the break-up of her marriage, the latest one. She was introduced to a 'guru', who impressed upon her the marvellous healing powers of total abstinence, in other words, total chastity, for two years! And, it worked.

If your suitor presses you for a firm commitment, in other words, he can't keep his hands off your body, tell him you've now joined this religious sect, and it is forbidden for you to be physically involved with anyone, for a long time yet . . . it's all to do with your personal problem, and your 'guru', who instructs you, is helping you overcome this very big mental worry. He'll look surprised and want to know what problem, and why don't you ask me to help?

You then tell him gently that he is the problem. When you explain to him that you see him as a father figure, have a fixation about it, he might well – considering he's six years younger than you – go into shock.

Confide in him, you want to call him Daddy, and cuddle up to him, and that is why your 'guru' is helping you to overcome this problem, and under no circumstances must you get physically involved with anyone for the time being.

If he comes out of the shock, and can still talk, he will do one of two things; he will have nothing more to do with you, so your honour will be intact. OR he'll be so fascinated by your revelation that he will want to study your case, and forget his personal interest.

Either way you win!

✷ ✷ ✷ ✷ ✷ ✷ ✷ ✷ ✷ ✷

A young psychiatrist was telling an older colleague about his troubles in getting intelligent responses from his patients.

'Suppose you ask me some of your questions,' the older one suggested.

'Well, my first question is this: What is it that wears the skirt and from those lips comes pleasure?'

'A Scot blowing bagpipes,' the veteran replied.

'Right,' said the younger man. 'Now what is it that has smooth curves and at an unexpected moment becomes uncontrollable?'

'A good man's bowling.'

'Right. What do you think of when two arms slip round your shoulder?'

'Why, a rugby tackle,' replied the older colleague.

'Right,' said the young psychiatrist, 'all your answers were absolutely correct, but you'd be surprised at the silly answers I keep getting!'

⊙ ⊙ ⊙ ⊙ ⊙ ⊙ ⊙ ⊙ ⊙ ⊙

Egotists

An egotist is a man with an inflated opinion of his own import-ance. Unfortunately he inflicts this outsize ego on some poor female, who has been trapped, mesmerized or hypnotized into becoming his life's partner, and she accepts, deluding herself, she will change him into a human being; alas, the divorce courts are stacked with evidence to the contrary.

An egotist labours under the misapprehension that he has been cheated out of his just rewards. These men reach a certain position, a plateau in life, but haven't the talent, ability, or personality to go any further. Second rate themselves, they resent anyone else who makes it to the top.

Your egotist is found in all walks of life. For example: A TV presenter, with a small measure of success in a local show. His appearance, personality, is only just adequate, he doesn't make much of an impact, so his resentment is shown in petty little acts. An artiste, with a personality that puts him in the shade, is quickly 'on' n' 'off'. If it's a big name person, he will ingratiate himself with the visiting star.

He never praises someone who has made it big-time. He feels someone is not giving his tiny talent a proper chance!

Take another case, a store manager, who treats his staff like dirt. Ticks them off in front of people, or, like one manager I met, totally ignores the staff, unless they confront him or it is necessary.

He toadies up to the 'top brass', hoping for that big pro-motion he so richly deserves. The egotist always blames others. Fate, people, wife, it's never his fault that his marvel-lous qualities haven't been fully appreciated.

He battles for the limelight, 24 hours a day; it's a full time career, concentrating upon yourself. He can never get enough attention, praise or appreciation, like a spoilt child he demands that the spotlight be on him constantly.

If you are seriously thinking of a permanent, or even a trial association, with an egomaniac, be warned, you're in for a very bumpy ride. What he needs is not a wife, or partner, but to take out a mortgage on another mirror. How can anyone compete with a man who is having a love affair with himself?

There's no room for a stranger, and that is what you will always be.

His vanity is enormous.

You shovel on flattery by the bucketful, he'll wallow in it. For birthdays, give him one of two presents. Give him another mirror, or ask for him to get some more pictures taken (OK, so he had a bunch done 3 months ago). Get the check-out girl, at your local supermarket, to ask him for one, the lady in the bakery shop, and anyone else who can use a bit of cash; bribery is still in fashion, thank heaven. Tell him they all want his picture, he won't turn a hair, just accept it as the norm. And, remind him you have only 15 pictures of him in your apartment, you could use one more.

They – the egotists – take themselves seriously. He'll not wonder why strangers should want his picture, his ego prevents any kind of realistic sense from seeping in; it's a form of protective oil, a covering that nature gives all sensitive men like himself.

If you are still determined to go ahead and persevere with your egotist, then I must, to maintain a clear conscience, give you this advice. Enrol at your local Polytech for a course in 'SYCOPHANCY', it's absolutely marvellous, and pays good dividends, some of the results have been quite interesting. A lady in Texas did just that.

The course consists of such lessons as the following:

'HOW TO FLATTER' – HOW TO SUCK UP TO YOUR EGOTIST – HOW TO PAMPER and PAMPER (a 24 hour chore).
HOW TO DISPLAY UNFLAGGING ENTHUSIASM AT HEARING THE SAME OLD STORY AGAIN AND AGAIN.
HOW TO PRAISE YOUR EGOMANIAC, WHEN FEELING FED-UP.
HOW TO FLATTER, AND LOOK SINCERE (Very popular course).

These are some of the topics, there are more. The lady from Texas graduated with honours. Subjected to his cheating, tantrums, she put up with a great deal, but one day she decided she'd had enough.

Her husband lay dying, and wanted to settle affairs, to make a clean breast of things, to make amends for the way he had treated his wife.

'MaryLou,' he whispered, 'Ah just get some things

112

offa ma chest, You well remember that robbery we had, an' you lost 100,000 dollars that was – stolen, it was no robbery, honey, it was me . . . can you ever forgive me?'

'Shush,' she said softly, 'it's alright, Joe.'

'No, MaryLou, I just gotta have everything offa ma chest. That week I up 'n told you ah was in New Orleans on business. I was with Jennie Baker, your old school friend, we was having an affair. And that time the police picked you up for drunken driving . . . it was ME that tipped them off . . . Oh, can you ever, ever forgive me MaryLou . . .?'

MaryLou patted his hand gently, 'Hush now, don't you go frettin' yourself, sweetheart,' she said 'it was little 'ole me that put strychnine in your chili con carne . . .'

All women do not go to these lengths, but British wives can do unexpected things too.

Diane had been married for many weary years to her pompous husband; years of sarcastic remarks in public, tantrums over a shirt, displays of unbelievable childishness, always the 'I – ME – I' to the forefront.

Then it was his birthday, once again Diane arranged every thing. Caterers, flowers, drinks, music and guest list, no expense was spared, until she suggested a new dress for the occasion. He exploded, wasn't it costing the earth already without her wanting to make it even more expensive? Her blue dress was more than adequate.

It was a splendid affair. Business colleagues and friends congratulated their host on a superb turn-out. They drank champers, ate the smoked salmon, caviare. Tucked into the buffet, it was past three before the last guest left.

Next day, the house resembling a battleground, Oliver went as usual to his office.

Arriving home that evening, anticipating a quiet dinner, in his well-run house, he was astounded to find the battleground just as he had left it that morning, also a letter, a short one.

'You might notice that I'm no longer around, and don't intend to be again. I shan't bother to explain, you wouldn't know or understand. I've bought some new clothes long overdue, a short mink jacket, I'm taking the Mini, been to the bank, and drawn a sizeable cheque, also long overdue.

113

I do hope you and yourself will be very happy together.

Diane.

Many a young bride has walked down the aisle, with stars in her eyes, hope in her heart, thinking she will be able to change her egotist. Sadly, what mother has ruined, stays ruined. Think once! twice! three times! then, if you've got courage, say – No.

* * * * * * * * * *

Bernard Shaw's criticism of the marriage ritual:

'When two people are under the influence of the most violent, most insane, most delusive and transient of passions, they are required to solemnly swear they will remain in that excited abnormal and exhausting condition continuously until death do them part.'

☉ ☉ ☉ ☉ ☉ ☉ ☉ ☉ ☉ ☉

Final Thoughts

Sharing your life with a fellow doesn't have to be impossible or a marathon test, indeed once you find the key to what makes him tick you are in the driving seat, only never let him know that, that's why this 'equality' talk is such rubbish.

There is no such thing as equality between a man and a woman. Both are different, equal in special ways. Man has his qualities, woman has her weapons, *vive lé différence* and who would have it any other way. Think of the fun, excitement, to say nothing of the pleasure that happens between a civilized man and a woman.

Patience is essential in handling a man. After all, many of the species we meet today could have come straight out of the cave. They eat like the original caveman, they behave like a man still wearing a loin cloth, but many a cave-wife had complete control over her cave, because the little woman used her nut (brain).

When he came home in a brutal mood, she played it cool. 'Forsooth, Cedric, thou art indeed bushed this day.' Grunt! grunt! 'My brave hunter is tired and hungry, lie thee down upon thy Armadillo blanket and thy doting woman will give thee food.'

The clever girl then gives him a steaming bowl of brontosaurus soup, laced with a liberal helping of bromide-plectaridoral, a powder which did wonders for the disposition. It calmed the brute down, sent a warm glow through his body and by the time she served him a roasted leg of lion, four dinosaur steaks and a couple of chickens as dessert, he was just a big playful puppy-dog, gentle and completely relaxed.

Makes sense, of course.

A soothing powder works miracles with babies, so it applies also to the grown-up ones. It's a skill that has been used since the beginning of time itself.

The apothecary has been kept busy since way back. Cleopatra had one on hand working around the clock sometimes calming Caesar, or Mark Anthony, or her other playmates. Catherine the Great, Marie Antoinette, Madame du Barry Pompadour, all these ladies relied upon the skill of the apoth-

116

ecary to see them through many a problem, which the male would inflict upon them from time to time.

Different women use different methods.

A Greek peasant woman told her daughter. 'Eat before he comes home. Fill him up with a good meal as soon as he enters the house. Keep your troubles to yourself, let him eat, drink a glass of wine, relax . . . let him take his time . . . then you can do anything you wish with him.'

So, mon ami, study the brute and take whatever action you deem necessary.

A child has the very last word.

Johnny's father brought his boss home for dinner, a gruff, very self-centred man. He was the perfect carica-ture of all the jests, the jokes that are made about bosses.

During the dinner Johnny stared at the visitor through-out the meal. Unable to stand it any longer the guest spoke, 'Tell me, why is it that you are staring so hard at me?'

The boy replied, 'My Dad says that you are a self-made man.' The Boss beamed with pleasure, and proudly he admitted that this was indeed true. Then with the utmost candour of the young, Johnny said, 'But why did you make yourself like that?'

If you don't like the result, change the image.

⊙ ⊙ ⊙ ⊙ ⊙ ⊙ ⊙ ⊙ ⊙ ⊙

PRESS QUOTES

"One of the funniest books I've read in years .... had me in stitches..."
J. Hughes — C. Journal

"Marvellously funny ..... a MUST for anyone's reading .....
great present"
TVAM

"No one is spared — Irish, Scots, Welsh, Foreigners ... HOW TO HANDLE A MAN, just about covers the lot...! A tonic, should be in every girl's bedroom ... fun and funny...."
Western Mail

"Brynn knows how to humour them'... its all tongue in cheek. Saucy and salacious...' Blend of good old-fashioned fun'n spice without porn . . . refreshingly funny..."
Belfast Telegraph

"She sends up the fellows something rotten, the text is all in fun with a strong ring of truth... but its very clear she adores men, when she is not pinpointing their weakness's. From the EGOTIST to the LECHER, Brynn moves in and dissects ... a family book, enjoyable fun..."
Evening Post

"Highly critical of the TAFF'S, the JOCKS, PADDIES for their arrogant superior attitudes towards women. Brynn says, "They seem to think because they are biologically equipped differently from us, they also have a better brain. "she grins and winks finding the whole subject amusing and enjoyable."
B. Roberts, Glasgow

Bretonn Associates Ltd.
P.O. Box 652
Gorseinon, Nr. Swansea. SA4 3WN.
Wales.

'Faith and Positive Thinking'
'Stop Feeling Sorry for Yourself'

Coming Soon
'Let's Have a Pity Party'

A Light-hearted Look at Men!

Men are part of this world we females inhabit.

Man was made for woman, woman the perfect half of man as nature intended. If however, a girl finds she's been unlucky in her choice of male in the 'Lucky dip of life' and is landed with the chauvinistic specimen, never fear, there are ways of handling the most revolting type of chauvinistic pig.

A guide-line to the different types of male in Britain and overseas will help the uninitiated, the innocent, the virgin.

THE MESSAGE IS BRIEFLY - DON'T GIVE UP!

Male chasing female – female using her charms and other weapons in handling a male is still the greatest game in town, and until something better comes along, why not become an expert and have some laughs, some fun along the way.

For those of you still celebrating last Christmas,-or- looking forward to the Christmas ahead, I send this little poem, to greet you. To remind all of us it is a time of peace and goodwill toward all —Men!

....

'Twas' the night before Christmas, and all through the house..
the whole damn family wuz drunken than a louse.....
Granma and Granpa decked out in leather 'n chains....
watching the kids beating out each other's brains...!

Ma wuz home from the Cathouse....there wuz me outa jail...
had settled upstairs losing no time on my bail....
When out on the lawn there arose such a clatter....
I just jumped outa bed to see what wuz the matter....

Straight to the window I made a fast pass, threw it wide
open... and fell out on my ass....
And what to my bloodshot eyes should appear....
but a rusty old sleigh and a dozen reindeer....
with a little old driver clutching his stick....
Ah jus' knowed right away that the drunkard was Nick!

Slower than snails his reindeer they came....
He shouted 'n swore as he called them by name....
"Now Prancer, Now Dancer...move on up over the roof...
'n shift your fat backsides or I'll cut off your hoofs...."

When up on the roof Nick stumbled 'n fell....
and came down the chimney like a Bat out of hell....
Nick staggered and stumbled and went to the door....
tripped over a beer bottle and fell flat on the floor.
I heard him exclaim as he drove out of sight...

'Oh! Pish on you all...and a bloody goodnight...!!!

....

Illustrations by Lynic